Cléo de 5 à 7

CINÉ-FILES: The French Film Guides
Series Editor: Ginette Vincendeau

From the pioneering days of the Lumière brothers' Cinématographe in 1895, France has been home to perhaps the most consistently vibrant film culture in the world, producing world-class directors and stars, and a stream of remarkable movies, from popular genre films to cult avant-garde works. Many of these have found a devoted audience outside France, and the arrival of DVD is now enabling a whole new generation to have access to contemporary titles as well as the great classics of the past.

The Ciné-Files French Film Guides build on this welcome new access, offering authoritative and entertaining guides to some of the most significant titles, from the silent era to the early twenty-first century. Written by experts in French cinema, the books combine extensive research with the author's distinctive, sometimes provocative perspective on each film. The series will thus build up an essential collection on great French classics, enabling students, teachers and lovers of French cinema both to learn more about their favourite films and make new discoveries in one of the world's richest bodies of cinematic work.

Ginette Vincendeau

Published Ciné-Files
Alphaville (Jean-Luc Godard, 1965) – Chris Darke
Les Diaboliques (Henri-Georges Clouzot, 1955) – Susan Hayward
La Haine (Mathieu Kassovitz, 1995) – Ginette Vincendeau
La Reine Margot (Patrice Chéreau, 1994) – Julianne Pidduck

Forthcoming Ciné-Files include:
Amélie (Jean-Pierre Jeunet, 2001) – Isabelle Vanderschelden
Le Corbeau (Henri-Georges Clouzot, 1943) – Judith Mayne
Casque d'or (Jacques Becker, 1952) – Sarah Leahy
Cléo de 5 à 7 (Agnès Varda, 1962) – Valerie Orpen
La Règle du jeu (Jean Renoir, 1939) – Keith Reader
Rififi (Jules Dassin, 1955) – Alastair Phillips
La Grande illusion (Jean Renoir, 1937) – Martin O'Shaughnessy
Un chien andalou (Luis Buñuel, 1929) – Elza Adamowicz
À bout de souffle (Jean-Luc Godard, 1960) – Ramona Fotiade

Cléo de 5 à 7

(Agnès Varda, 1961)

Valerie Orpen

I.B. TAURIS

LONDON · NEW YORK

Published in 2007 by I.B.Tauris & Co. Ltd

6 Salem Road, London W2 4BU

175 Fifth Avenue, New York NY 10010

ibtauris.com

ISBN: 978 1 84511 369 8

A full CIP record for this book is available from the British Library

Typeset in Minion by Dexter Haven Associates Ltd, London
Printed and bound in Great Britain by TJ International Ltd, Padstow, Cornwall

Contents

Acknowledgements | vii

Synopsis | ix

Map | xi

Introduction | 1

1   Production contexts | 3

    Agnès Varda's career up to *Cléo de 5 à 7*, | 3
    or the game of art and chance

    The genesis of *Cléo de 5 à 7* | 6

    Agnès Varda and *Cléo de 5 à 7* in the | 11
    context of the New Wave

    Historical contexts: the backdrop | 16
    of the Algerian war

2   Structure, style and themes | 22

    An unusual narrative structure: 13 | 22
    chapters in 'real' time

    A 'subjective documentary': focalisation, | 30
    character interiority and realism

    The Spoilt Child, the Maid-cum-Madam and | 38
    the Chatterbox: characters in *Cléo de 5 à 7*

    Cléo de 5 à 7 as a filmic illustration of the | 48
    Existentialist zeitgeist

    The loneliness of the *flâneuse* | 55

      Paris: city of light and enlightenment   63

      Nature and death   66

      Nudity and costume, truth and masks   70

3   Reception   81

      Box office and reviews   81

      A feminist film?   87

      Conclusion   95

      Appendix 1: Film credits   97

      Appendix 2: Chapter breakdown   99

      Appendix 3: Filmography   101

      Appendix 4: Selected bibliography   103

      Index   107

Acknowledgements

My first thanks go to Ginette Vincendeau for giving me this opportunity to write about *Cléo de 5 à 7*, for her enthusiasm and patience, as well as her usual invaluable and generous guidance, feedback and loan of books and difficult-to-find material. Thank you also to Phillipa Brewster for accepting the project, and to Susan Lawson for her help with the illustrations and to Gretchen Ladish for her painstaking and valuable editorial assistance.

My research was greatly facilitated by the staff at the Bibliothèque du Film (BiFi) in Paris, the British Film Institute (BFI) in London, the Forum des Images in Paris (and Pauline Husy in particular), the Bibliothèque Nationale François Mitterrand in Paris, and the British Library.

I am also very grateful to Jonathan Lewsey, Alastair Phillips, Michael Temple, Isabelle Vanderschelden, James Williams and Piotr Zrajkowski for drawing my attention to, or providing, relevant books, articles, DVDs and videotapes; Ute Bauermeister for her expertise on Rainer Maria Rilke; Luke Scofield and Fiona Ponikwer for their help and erudition on the *flâneur*; Fiona additionally for her knowledge of tarots; Julien Planté for inviting me to introduce *Cléo de 5 à 7* at the French Institute in London in June 2005; Isabelle Méda for her generous gifts of books courtesy of Gallimard; Abdellah Chouaib for his knowledge of Arab superstitions; Anne Martina and Clément Oudart for their Paris flats, which pleasantly facilitated part of my research and allowed me to retrace Cléo's footsteps; and Henning Transgaard for commenting on the project. Last but not least, thank you to my former students at the University of Manchester (1999–2002), who loved *Cléo* and encouraged me to write a book about it.

Synopsis

Cléo de 5 à 7, directed by Agnès Varda in 1961 and released in 1962, chronicles 90 minutes in the life of rising pop singer Cléo Victoire (Corinne Marchand) with three singles to her credit. She has an abdominal tumour and is awaiting the results of a biopsy to know whether or not it is malignant. Fearing the worst, she seeks reassurance and solace from a variety of characters. The film opens with Cléo visiting a fortune-teller, who reads cards and also her palm, though she refuses to comment on the latter. Neither reading is reassuring to Cléo, who interprets the fortune-teller's final silence as an omen of death. Cléo then walks to a nearby café to meet her housekeeper and confidante, Angèle (Dominique Davray), and tell her about the reading. Cléo hysterically breaks down and Angèle has to calm her down. After having a coffee, they leave the café and enter a hatter's nearby on the rue de Rivoli. Cléo tries on many hats and finally purchases a pointed fur number. She wants to wear it straightaway, but Angèle, who is keenly superstitious, forbids her, telling her it will bring her bad luck. They take a taxi driven by a woman and wend their way south, across the Seine, to Cléo's home near Montparnasse. They alternately chat to the driver, look out of the windows at Parisian life and listen to a radio news broadcast. Back at home, Cléo changes into a négligée and is visited by her lover, José (José Luis de Vilallonga), who can see her only briefly, and by her composer, Bob (Michel Legrand), and songwriter, Plumitif (Serge Korber), whom she has summoned for a last-minute rehearsal. A new song, 'Un Cri d'Amour', causes her to break down and to argue with Bob and Angèle. She decides to change into a black dress and go out alone, wearing the black hat, despite Angèle's warnings of impending doom. She walks down to the corner and stops briefly at the Dôme café to have a brandy before moving on, past buskers who nauseate her, to a sculptor's studio where her friend Dorothée (Dorothée Blank) works as an artist's model. Dorothée offers Cléo a lift in her boyfriend Raoul's car, as she has to collect some film reels from Montparnasse station and drop them off at the cinema where Raoul (Raymond Cauchetier) works as a projectionist. When they get to the cinema, Raoul shows them a short burlesque film about a man who wrongly believes his girlfriend has died when she has only hurt herself, because his dark glasses made him see everything in a negative light. She takes leave of Dorothée, who recommends visiting the nearby Parc Montsouris. There, Cléo walks alone until she meets Antoine (Antoine Bourseiller), a soldier on leave from the Algerian war. He is about to return to the front and offers to accompany her to the hospital if she later accompanies him to the train station. The film ends when she learns the implicit diagnosis from the doctor, which paradoxically results in her feeling happy and relieved. Shot on location in Paris in June and July, the film charts Cléo's growing self-awareness and journey towards serenity as she wanders through the city. It is in black and white, except for the opening sequence, which is in colour. The full credits can be found in the Film credits (Appendix 1).

Map of Cléo's journey around Paris

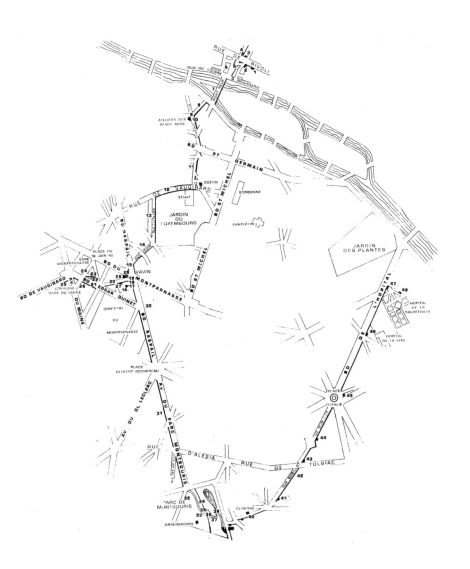

Introduction

Why *Cléo*?

Cléo de 5 à 7 isn't the best-known French film, nor is it for that matter the best-known French New Wave film. It may be one of the better-known French films directed by a woman, though possibly not in France, where it has probably been superseded by more recent offerings from Coline Serreau, Josiane Balasko or Agnès Jaoui. *Cléo* is nevertheless an important film: it was the only New Wave film directed by a woman. It is taught on many film and/or modern language undergraduate and postgraduate courses in Britain and the United States and is very popular with students, both male and female. I first discovered *Cléo* as an undergraduate and a decade later taught it on my French New Wave course at the University of Manchester.

I don't know many people who dislike *Cléo de 5 à 7*. It is cinematically quite complex and thematically grapples with a somewhat grim subject matter as well as some potentially profound philosophical concepts while deftly avoiding the pitfalls of pretentiousness and abstruseness. The plot is simple enough: a young woman is awaiting the results of a medical test. The linear time-frame is fantastically simple to follow and analyse. Yet the film withholds a certain amount of information, which is intriguing but also gives the viewers more freedom to draw their own conclusions. For instance, will Cléo die? Do all the omens in the film come true? How can a woman who is so professionally accomplished and who has such an entourage ultimately be so isolated and lonely in her (two) hour(s) of need?

Varda's place in French cinema history is also intriguing: both well known at home and abroad, yet often neglected in discussions of the New Wave, but perhaps not always – as has been argued – for misogynistic reasons. Furthermore, Varda has been both critiqued and championed by feminist film scholars.

Although I realise it has become quite commonplace for a female film scholar to discuss a film made by a female director and concerning a female protagonist, this was not something that I set out to do. My intention was simpler in that I wanted to analyse a film that I, as well as others, both male and female, enjoyed, and found rewarding to teach and study. Last but not least, the absence of studies on *Cléo de 5 à 7* seemed to me glaring and inexplicable. Assessing whether *Cléo* is, or not, a feminist film, will not be the central remit of this book, though I will nevertheless address issues of feminist content and reception in Chapters Two and Three respectively.

The film is divided into 13 chapters (see Appendix 2 for a chapter breakdown). In many cases, I will refer to chapter numbers rather than sequences. So as to distinguish between the chapters in this book and the film's chapters, the latter will be italicised. In the breakdown of the film, Part 1 designates the *Prologue–Chapter 7* inclusive. Part 2 designates the rest of the film.

All the film dates in this book are release dates.
All the translations from the French are mine unless otherwise indicated.
All shots in the close textual analyses are static unless otherwise stated.

1   Production contexts

Agnès Varda's career up to *Cléo de 5 à 7*, or the game of art and chance

Unlike most French New Wave directors, Agnès Varda was not predestined for a career in film-making. Her youth was characterised by geographical movement, change and art. Born on 30 May 1928 in Ixelles, a bohemian and artistic area of Brussels, to a French mother and a Greek father, Arlette Varda, as she was then known,[1] spent her childhood in Sète in the Languedoc-Roussillon region of the south of France; in her teens, she went to the lycée Victor Duruy in Paris and later briefly studied literature and psychology under the philosopher Gaston Bachelard at the Sorbonne. She then changed direction, switching to art history at the École du Louvre, with a view to becoming a museum curator. However, at this stage, Varda realised that she didn't really want to spend the rest of her life filing archives in provincial museums and opted for something more practical and hands-on. She took an evening class at the École de Vaugirard for a CAP ('Certificat d'Aptitude Professionnelle' – a vocational training certificate) in photography. Ignoring W.C. Fields' advice never to work with children or animals, her first jobs in the late 1940s involved taking photographic portraits of children, either in their environments, or with 'Father Christmas' in the Galeries Lafayette department store in Paris.[2]

Clearly, Varda was an artistic young woman, but who nevertheless kept her feet firmly on the ground. Her mother admired artists and had wanted Arlette, her third-born child out of five, to become one. Later, she liked to introduce her daughter not so much as a film-maker but as an artist. In Sète, Varda had befriended an artistic family. She followed the three daughters to

Paris, where they moved in the artistic circles of the Left Bank. One of the sisters married Jean Vilar, another *Sétois*, who became the director of the Avignon Theatre Festival (1947–1950) and later, the director of the renowned Théâtre National Populaire, or TNP (1951–1963), where Varda herself worked as the official stage photographer from 1951 to 1961. It was there that Varda met Philippe Noiret and Silvia Montfort, two stage actors with little or no experience of screen acting, but whom she would call upon to play the couple in her first film, *La Pointe courte* (1954–1956). After a few years at the TNP, Varda began to feel the limitations of still photography and tried her hand at the moving image. What is remarkable at this juncture is that, although Varda's technical abilities were undisputed, at least where the camera was concerned, she allegedly had virtually no experience of the cinema as a spectator. Varda claims that by her mid-twenties, she had seen only a handful of films in her life, including *Snow White and the Seven Dwarfs* (Disney Studios, 1937), Marcel Carné's *Quai des brumes/Port of Shadows* (1938) and *Les Enfants du paradis/Children of Paradise* (1945) and *L'Idiot* (Georges Lampin, 1946). Her case is unique in the context of the French New Wave where all her colleagues were film buffs and quite a few (the *Cahiers du cinéma* crowd) were erudite film critics. In her book, *Varda par Agnès*, she describes meeting the *Cahiers* film-makers through Alain Resnais, who was helping her edit *La Pointe courte*. She felt completely out of her depth as these young cinephiles animatedly discussed films and cited directors she had never even heard of. 'I was anomalous, I felt small and ignorant, and the only girl among the *Cahiers* boys'.[3] She later admitted that her ignorance was a blessing in disguise: 'If I had seen at the time films made by masters, either male or female, and which I have discovered since, I would perhaps have been intimidated or even inhibited'.[4] So although Varda could certainly wield a camera, she was oblivious to the context of her first film, and this may have been one of her greatest strengths.

There is something brazen, though perhaps unwittingly so, about Varda's entry into the film industry. In her chapter on the making of *La Pointe courte* in her book *Varda par Agnès*, Varda uses the word *hasard* ('chance' or 'accident') three times.[5] Despite enjoying her job at the TNP, Varda increasingly felt that still photography was 'too silent'.[6] The moving image also seemed to her to convey far more accurately two themes that recur in her work: the passage of time and the hiatus between subjective experience and objective description.[7] Varda's connection to Sète was re-established through her love for a fishing neighbourhood called La Pointe Courte, and also through her *Sétois* friends. One of these friends, who had moved to Paris, was dying of a brain tumour, and Varda decided that taking him down to Sète to shoot a film might cheer him up. Varda had inherited some money after her father's death and borrowed the rest. She established her own small production company, Ciné-Tamaris, and formed a cooperative with the cast and crew. Thanks largely to *hasard* and supportive personnel, the film cost just seven million francs, which represented one-tenth of the average budget for a 1954 French film and a quarter of the budget of later New Wave films such as François Truffaut's *Les Quatre cents coups/The 400 Blows* (1959) and Jean-Luc Godard's *À bout de souffle/Breathless* (1960).[8] Varda had no idea how to go about editing the resulting 10,000 metres of footage and called upon Alain Resnais, who had a few shorts under his belt and lived nearby. Reluctant at first, Resnais finally accepted and the two became good friends as well as members of the so-called 'Left Bank' sub-group of the New Wave. *La Pointe courte* was largely well received, though many critics disliked the stilted acting. Sadly, because the film was shot without the permission of the CNC (Centre National de la Cinématographie), it qualified as 'amateur' and could not be exhibited in commercial cinemas. It was shown briefly at the Cannes festival and then for a few weeks at a Paris 'art et essai' (repertory) cinema, the Studio Parnasse, but no distributor was interested.[9] Certainly, in its very low-budget production values and location-shooting aesthetics, the film anticipated the New Wave.

In a long and detailed 1974 interview, Varda explained that after making *La Pointe courte*, she still believed that the film was a one-off. 'I never thought of myself as a filmmaker.'[10] She kept her day job at the TNP, since *La Pointe courte* was not profitable. But three years later, the producer Pierre Braunberger invited her to make films for the tourist board. She wasn't overly keen at first, but realised that commissions would be her gateway to a career in film.[11] She made three shorts: *Ô saisons, ô châteaux!* (1957), a documentary in colour about the Loire *châteaux*; *L'Opéra-Mouffe* (1958), which could be described as a semi-autobiographical documentary, recording the altered and subjective viewpoint of a pregnant woman in the then-seedy neighbourhood of the rue Mouffetard (Varda was pregnant at the time); and *Du côté de la côte* (1958), a documentary about the French Riviera, or Côte d'Azur. Varda is also adamant, not just in this interview, but in many others, that being a woman never stood in the way of her newly chosen career path. 'I didn't ask myself if it would be difficult for me as a woman to make films; I must say I didn't start with an inferiority complex.'[12] She explains that her main hurdle was being too short and having to stand on chairs with her camera. With hindsight, she acknowledged the revolutionary production of *La Pointe courte* in the context of the extremely hierarchichal system at work in the French film industry of the 1950s, where personnel typically had to work their way up the ladder for many years before they could even hope to direct. Ironically,

Varda received the card entitling her to be a director ten years after making her first film...[13]

The genesis of *Cléo de 5 à 7*

After the three aforementioned commissioned shorts, Varda wanted to make a more personal feature-length fiction film. Originally, she wanted to shoot a colour film, *La Mélangite*, in Sète and Venice. But her producer, Georges de Beauregard (who produced other New Wave films, such as Jean-Luc Godard's 1959 *À bout de souffle*, as well as films peripheral to the New Wave, such as Jean-Pierre Melville's *Léon Morin Prêtre*, 1961, Jacques Demy's *Lola*, 1961, and Jacques Rozier's *Adieu Philippine*, 1962),[14] objected on financial grounds. 'Make a little black and white film that won't cost more than 32 million F,' he advised her.[15] Varda decided to shoot in Paris for practical and financial reasons. Paris as a city of fear also had a personal resonance for Varda: as a provincial girl arriving in the French metropolis, Varda had been afraid of the city and its dangers, afraid of getting lost, of feeling lonely and alienated.[16] But whereas, again, other New Wave film-makers' points of reference when filming in Paris were often other films shot in Paris, Varda's references were more literary and artistic. She cites the urban meanderings of the solitary Danish poet in Rainer Maria Rilke's *Notebook of Malte Laurids Brigge/Die Aufzeichnungen des Malte Laurids Brigge* (1910) and Diderot's 1796 picaresque novel *Jacques le fataliste* (which features a rather indolent master and a fatalistic servant in dialogue). Thematically, Varda refers to the modern preoccupation with cancer but also to the paintings of the sixteenth-century German artist Hans Baldung Grien, a contemporary of Dürer. One of his paintings in particular made a great impression on Varda: *Death Kissing a Maiden* (1517), a subject Dürer treated several times, depicts a young and beautiful naked woman threatened by a grotesque skeleton, who is sometimes shown pulling her long blonde hair.

From the outset, it was crucial to Varda that her protagonist should be a stereotypically beautiful young woman, almost a cliché. This was for both narrative and commercial reasons; death and illness are more shocking and poignant when they cut down people in their prime, but also, Varda lucidly believed that spectators would be less gripped by the plight of an older and less striking female character.[17] She chose Corinne Marchand for the lead role having seen her in husband-to-be Jacques Demy's *Lola* (1961), where she played a dancer. Marchand was a 23-year-old professional singer and dancer and *Cléo* was her first major role after half a dozen bit parts in largely minor films. She had been better known in America than in France: 'Photographers discovered the Marchand face and figure gracing the revue of "La Nouvelle Ève", the famous Paris nightclub, and put her smile on the pages of *Life*, *Esquire* and *Playboy*.'[18] Her first big break was not in cinema, but in the stage musical *Pacifico* (1958), where she played alongside Georges Guétary and Bourvil, and which was a runaway hit.[19] In terms of her appearance, Corinne Marchand was an exception in the New Wave: curvaceous and blonde. Actresses in New Wave films were very seldom blonde. Blondeness represented a clichéd and outdated form of stardom that belonged to the *cinéma de papa*, with Martine Carol, the top box office star before Brigitte Bardot (who dyed her hair blonde from 1953), being a prime example. For New Wave film-makers, blondeness was 'extraordinary' and artificial, and was therefore incompatible with the New Wave's more 'ordinary' and 'natural' characters (and actors). When it did appear, blondeness was used ironically or was reappropriated with a twist: in *À bout de souffle*, Jean Seberg is blonde, but she is a modern version of the blonde *femme fatale* and traitor, because her hair is cropped (and such shorn hair was still quite outrageous in the 1960s). When Jeanne Moreau dyed her hair platinum blonde for Jacques Demy's *La Baie des anges/Bay of Angels* in 1963, it was entirely for parodic reasons: a parody of blondeness/whiteness (she is also often dressed in white in the film), of excessive femininity, of trashy glamour. Finally, Godard sent up stellar blondeness in *Le Mépris/Contempt* (1963) by using Brigitte Bardot for the central role; he soon demolished her trademark blondeness, thus divesting her of her star persona, by covering her ostentatious mane with a wig, a short, dark bob, reminiscent of Anna Karina's hairdo. However, note that in *Cléo de 5 à 7* it is not just Cléo who is blonde; Anna Karina's character in the short film-within-the-film, though still recognisable as Karina, is also blonde.

Lola was the source of two more actors: Alan Scott, who played the male lead Frankie in *Lola*, plays a sailor in the short burlesque film in *Cléo*; Dorothée Blank had already worked with Varda in *L'Opéra-Mouffe*, but had also had a bit part in *French Cancan* (Jean Renoir, 1955), and played Dolly in *Lola* and a prostitute in both Godard's *Une femme est une femme/A Woman is a Woman* (1961) and later, in Demy's *Les Parapluies de Cherbourg/The Umbrellas of Cherbourg* (1964). Michel Legrand, who plays Bob, was better known as a prolific film composer associated, to a large extent, with the New Wave; a precocious virtuoso pianist and highly regarded jazz musician, his meeting with Jacques Demy was decisive in his career.[20] He wrote the score for *Lola*, and would be responsible for the scores of several of Demy's films (*La Baie des anges*; *Les Parapluies de Cherbourg*; *Les Demoiselles de Rochefort/The Young Girls of Rochefort*, 1967), which are still internationally popular, as well as several of Godard's films (*Une femme est une femme*, 1961, *Vivre sa vie/My Life to Live*, 1962, and *Bande à part/Band of Outsiders*, 1964), and Chris Marker's *Le Joli Mai* (1962). He would go on to work with a number of American and British directors as well, including Norman Jewison, for whom he wrote the score to *The Thomas Crown Affair* (1968), Joseph Losey (*The Go-Between*, 1970) and Robert Mulligan (*The Summer of '42*, 1971). It is interesting to note that Varda chose a melodist for the score of *Cléo de 5 à 7*, rather than an experimental or atonal composer such as Pierre Barbaud (who had worked on *La Pointe courte*, and would go on to write the scores for her later films *Les Créatures*, *Ulysse* and *7p., cuis., s. de b.,… à saisir*) or Joanna Bruzdowicz (*Sans toit ni loi/Vagabond*, *Kung-Fu master!*, *Jacquot de Nantes*, *Les Glaneurs et la glaneuse*, and *Les Glaneurs et la glaneuse… deux ans après*). This is entirely appropriate to the film and particularly the character of Cléo. The score will be analysed in depth in Chapter Two.

Finally, Varda called upon Dominique Davray to play Angèle, Antoine Bourseiller for the role of the soldier Antoine and José Luis de Vilallonga for the part of Cléo's *amant* ('lover'), José. Mainly a comedy actress, Davray had played Julie in *Casque d'or/Golden Helmet* (Jacques Becker, 1952) and small parts in Hitchcock's *To Catch a Thief* (1954) and Jean Delannoy's *Maigret tend un piège/Maigret Sets a Trap* (1958). For the part of Antoine, Varda wanted someone to whom she was personally close: Antoine Bourseiller, a film and stage actor, as well as a theatre director, had been involved in *Ô saisons, ô châteaux!* and *L'Opéra-Mouffe*, and is the father of Varda's daughter Rosalie. Varda even auditioned Demy, but decided against him because 'the tip of his nose and his cheerful eyes made him look too comical for a young soldier'.[21] José Luis de Vilallonga was somehow destined to be 'l'Amant'; his first role had been Jeanne Moreau's polo-playing lover, Raoul Flores, in Louis Malle's *succès de scandale* film *Les Amants/The Lovers* (1958). Varda wanted a traditional – if not parodic – lover figure, 'un amant de bibliothèque rose'.[22] He is very much a secondary character. In the script, Varda describes him as 'décoratif',[23] but he is nevertheless a good male yardstick against which to measure the more complex character of Antoine. De Vilallonga would later play another tanned, suave and stereotypical (as well as feckless) lover opposite Audrey Hepburn in *Breakfast at Tiffany's* (Blake Edwards, 1961). Last but not least, there were the actors in the small burlesque film who belonged to the New Wave set: the mythical Godard–Karina couple, Jean-Claude Brialy, Eddie Constantine, Danièle Delorme, Sami Frey and Yves Robert. The inspiration for the short film-within-the-film was Jean-Luc Godard's eyes. Varda had noticed that Godard always wore dark glasses (this is noticeable in his other cameo appearances, in Rohmer's *Le Signe du lion/The Sign of*

Leo, 1959, Rivette's *Le Coup du berger/Fool's Mate*, 1956, and *Paris nous appartient/Paris is Ours*, 1960, and in his own *À bout de souffle*). He once removed them and she noticed how beautiful his eyes were.[24] Hence this part where she succeeded in making him reveal his eyes.

There is something rather Bressonian about Varda's use of actors, and this is something that Jean-Michel Frodon has identified and approved of: '[These actors] are fantastic on screen, but one never wants to see them again in another film, because what they do seems to belong to that particular film.'[25] Robert Bresson used to call the actors in his film 'models'; they were non-professionals, and he would use them only once, because he believed that after one film, they had become 'tainted'. Although Varda has never professed that particular belief, and although most of the actors in her films have been professionals, she does like to use non-professionals (a couple of examples are Loye Payen, who plays Madame Irma, and Claire Drouot, who plays the wife Thérèse in *Le Bonheur/Happiness*; she was in fact the real-life wife of the actor Jean-Claude Drouot, who plays her husband François in *Le Bonheur*), or budding actors, and sometimes only once (like Corinne Marchand). Given that *Cléo de 5 à 7* is possibly one of the few films Marchand is remembered for, one may wonder to what extent Varda's casting choices have been detrimental to her actors' careers.

Varda originally wanted to call the film *La Petite Fille* – a reference to Cléo's vulnerability and the way she is fussed over and mollycoddled, yet ultimately left to face her fears alone. However, the tall, curvaceous and statuesque Corinne Marchand, despite her youth, was not sufficiently child-like (unlike another contemporary blonde, the sex-kittenish and Lolita-esque Brigitte Bardot); rather, she evoked the great seductresses and courtesans of history in Varda's mind, women like Liane de Pougy and Cléo de Mérode, both late nineteenth-, early twentieth-century dancers, and of course the ancient Egyptian empress Cleopatra.[26] Varda decided on a title that would refer to both the character and a precise time, between 5 and 7 p.m. She also wanted the title *Cléo de 5 à 7* to contain a teasing double-entendre: in French, a 'cinq à sept' traditionally designates the two-hour late afternoon slot when married men meet their mistresses, or more generally an afternoon lovers' tryst. Yet, this double entendre is also cruel, for we soon realise that Cléo's tryst may well be with Death.

Varda had planned filming to begin on 21 March 1961, the first day of spring. Financial setbacks meant that it had to be delayed by three months. At the time, Varda was distraught by this hitch, because she had wanted to capture Paris in the spring, reinforcing the dualism of renewal/birth and disease/death.[27] Yet, this setback turned out to be highly, and uncannily, fortuitous, both cinematographically (the longest, and possibly brightest, day of the year) and thematically. It allowed Antoine to utter the line about Gemini and Cancer in *Chapter 11*, prompting Cléo's angry reaction to a word that she cannot bear to hear, and it highlighted the transition from a metaphorically irresponsible youth (spring) to a more mature and serene adulthood (summer). *Cléo* was shot in black and white 35mm film (except for the credits sequence, which is in Eastmancolor) in June and July 1961, strictly in the chronological order of the script, something that is quite unusual (though Demy did the same with all his films).[28] Corinne Marchand commented on the experience of the chronological shoot, which she found very interesting, but sometimes difficult because her behaviour needed to change gradually, progressing from the more stilted to the more natural. It was also physically very realistic with Marchand looking increasingly tired and drawn.[29] Many scenes were shot at the exact diegetic time, so if a chapter states that the action is taking place between 17.45 and 17.52, we may glimpse a street clock showing that time.[30] This also meant that the light was as realistic as possible; the realism of locations and lighting was paramount to Varda: this was to be, after all, a 'subjective documentary'.[31]

Certainly, *Cléo de 5 à 7* is remarkably realist in its locations. The entire film was shot on location in the exact streets of the narrative. Even the short burlesque film, entitled *Les Fiancés du Pont MacDonald* (unnamed in the film), was shot on the banks of the Canal Saint-Denis near the Porte de la Villette, overlooked by the Boulevard MacDonald. However, despite the location shooting, which was not at all typical of silent cinema, it was shot in 1:33 ratio and at 16 frames per second to make it look speeded up. *Cléo de 5 à 7* was filmed in mostly natural daylight, since the narrative unfolds on a June afternoon. A diurnal Paris was quite typical of New Wave cinema, largely for practical and budgetary reasons. Thanks to the availability of handheld cameras and fast film stock, which was highly sensitive to existing light, directors of photography could shoot without the need for expensive additional lighting, though film quality and definition often suffered as a result. Location shooting consequently became the norm. However, some degree of artifice was still present. The interior of Cléo's loft-style apartment, for instance, which is diegetically supposed to be situated at no. 6, rue Huyghens, in Montparnasse (south of Paris), was in fact not a real abode but a disused stage-set hangar in Belleville to the north-east of Paris.[32] However, this was still a 'real' location and not a studio set. In addition, Varda liked to insert personal objects and possessions in her films; Cléo's jewellery, rocking chair and seven cats in fact belonged to Varda. She employed the production designer Bernard Évein for the interiors. Évein is associated with Demy's films (particularly the glorious colours in *Les Parapluies de Cherbourg* and *Les Demoiselles de Rochefort*). He worked on many New Wave films (Chabrol's *Les Cousins*, 1959; Godard's *Une femme est une femme*, 1961 and was set decorator on Truffaut's *Les Quatre cents coups*, but he remained loyal to Demy right up to his last film, *Trois places pour le 26* (1988). *Cléo de 5 à 7* was his only collaboration with Varda. Although Évein had to work in black and white for financial reasons (as he had done also for *Lola*), he made excellent use of the remarkable white apartment, contrasting it with dark, heavy and baroque furniture. The contrasts within Cléo's space are completely appropriate; on the one hand we have excessively 'girly' details: the garden swing, angel wings on the wall, thick rugs, fluffy kittens and ostrich feathers, but on the other, we have a vast, white and glacial space that reverberates with emptiness. This feminine clutter reminiscent of a Watteau painting becomes absorbed by the apartment's space and nihilistic whiteness.

Cléo de 5 à 7 was quite revolutionary in terms of its sound. As Betsy Ann Bogart has noted, 'In the history of sound recording in French cinema, *Cléo* plays an important role in the evolution from post-synchronized sound to on-location recording.'[33] This was in contrast to many New Wave films, which had to be post-synchronised, such as *À bout de souffle* and *Lola*. Some moments in *Cléo* had to be post-synchronised because their sound quality was too poor, such as the scene in the car after Dorothée and Cléo have left Montparnasse station and are on their way to Raoul's cinema. The availability of improved portable Nagra tape recorders was very fortuitous: the film's documentary aspect relies heavily on realistic sound. 'Nearly every image has its corresponding sound, including the kittens' meowing in Cléo's apartment, chisels of art students working on sculptures in the studio, snatches of conversations from passers-by, and birdsong and the waterfall in the Parc Montsouris.'[34] This said, some sounds are manipulated to express the character's aural point of view, such as the heightened sound of footsteps or ticking clocks, which will be discussed in Chapter Two.

Agnès Varda and *Cléo de 5 à 7* in the context of the New Wave

Varda has often been dubbed 'the mother',[35] or even 'the grandmother', of the New Wave,[36] and it is now generally acknowledged that *La Pointe courte* heralded the New Wave in terms of both production methods and aesthetics.[37] However, unlike other New Wave film-makers, Varda did not set out to break with past or existing cinema traditions; her first film was not a manifesto like *À bout de souffle*, there was no rebellious streak in her urge to make movies. In other words, while some of her New Wave peers were rebelling against the *cinéma du papa* ('daddy's cinema'), Varda was barely aware of it. Similarly, just as Varda did not intentionally or consciously make New Wave films, nor did she intentionally or consciously make feminist films, or at least not until later in her career. Nevertheless, many scholars and critics have acknowledged Varda's feminist legacy right from the start. Thus, Varda wasn't even consciously rebelling against *patriarchal* cinema, or at any rate, she claims that she wasn't intimidated by this very male-dominated world.[38] It is arguably this tunnel vision and artistic self-confidence that has enabled Varda to plough ahead and be accepted and embraced in a masculine and cinephile universe.

It was not just Varda's film-making practices that launched and/or espoused New Wave values; it was also her concept of *cinécriture* (a portmanteau noun, blending *cinéma* and *écriture*, or 'cinewriting') that was uncannily analogous to Alexandre Astruc's idea of the *caméra-stylo* (camerapen) (though, again, Varda claims she had no prior knowledge of Astruc's essay). Astruc's 1948 essay championed a more personal, 'written' cinema as well as the conception of a cinematic language in any discussion of film as an art.[39] Similarly, Varda believed that no distinction should be made between the script of a film and its style: 'To write a film is not a screenplay, but the creation of the film itself. What I do in the editing room is writing. Deciding [on the] music is part of the writing.'[40] Of course, for *Cléo*, Varda did more than just 'decide' on the music; she actually wrote the lyrics to all the songs, 'La Belle P...', 'La Menteuse' and 'Un Cri d'Amour', which became a hit on the film's release.[41] In the 1980s, Varda's films, for example *Sans toit ni loi* (1985), would bear the signature 'cinécrit par Agnès Varda'. This was certainly accurate: *Sans toit ni loi* was not 'written and directed' since there was no written script. Nor was it merely directed, since Varda's input was noticeable at every level. From the outset, Varda had been the total *auteur*, and all her films could have been signed thus.

The French New Wave has often been split, some may say arbitrarily, into two groups: the so-called 'Right Bank' *Cahiers du cinéma* critics (comprising in the main François Truffaut, Jean-Luc Godard, Claude Chabrol, Éric Rohmer and Jacques Rivette) and the 'Left Bank' group (Alain Resnais, Chris Marker and Agnès Varda – sometimes William Klein is also included). Most film scholars tend to neglect the latter group, treating it as merely a sub-group. James Monaco, in his book *The New Wave*, focuses almost exclusively on the *Cahiers* group and mentions Varda just twice in passing.[42] Claire Clouzot, on the other hand, considers the Left Bank film-makers as a distinct group *in opposition* to the New Wave.[43] Left Bank film-makers did indeed share certain formal, thematic and socio-political preoccupations. They all lived on the Left Bank in Paris. They were all inspired by an artistic eclecticism (but then, so was Godard, as Flitterman-Lewis has pointed out),[44] and the flow of mental processes. Preoccupations with time, memory and narration certainly do recur in the films of Varda, Resnais and Marker. But on the other hand, New Wave film-makers didn't care for these labels: Varda claims that the so-called 'Left Bank' group were simply friends who shared a love of travel and cats.[45] Varda on the face of it may seem to be the odd one out (the only woman; the only non-film buff) but in fact bridges both groups nicely. She shared affinities with both, and certainly displayed the same tenacity and *culot* ('cheek') as her *Cahiers* peers. She could have made Claude Chabrol's provocative line hers: 'All you need to know about making films can be learned in four hours.'[46] Furthermore, Godard's part in *Cléo*'s short film-within-the-film may have had less to do with his beautiful eyes than with some surprisingly common ground.

Godard is the only New Wave film-maker who gets an entry in the *abécédaire* at the beginning of her book, *Varda par Agnès* (besides Jacques Demy, of course…).[47] Yet, at first glance, Godard and Varda seem exact opposites: a wild child from the Swiss bourgeoisie and an ordinary girl from Brussels/Sète. He was the ultimate cinephile, she knew little about film when making her first movie. His first feature was an overt and provocative manifesto against the Tradition of Quality and was an immediate box office success (though not always a critical one, particularly with *Positif*); her first film was initially made for a friend and released in just one cinema, but those critics who saw it were generally impressed. Yet their films, especially in the early 1960s, uncannily mirror each other, and this for three reasons: their films are 1) driven by verbal language; 2) topical; 3) culturally eclectic. One could even add their common interest in Existentialism, but Truffaut also displayed this fashionable interest in *Tirez sur le pianiste/Shoot the Pianist* (1960). Certainly, Godard and Varda have more in common than Godard and Truffaut, who soon drifted apart in their film-making practices and ultimately fell out in the 1970s. Although Varda explained in 1974 how different she felt from Godard politically because she didn't want to put the working class on a pedestal ('I still participate in a bourgeois culture in which a film is made by an artist'),[48] at the beginning of their careers, they certainly shared much common ground and this is noticeable if we compare *À bout de souffle* and *Cléo de 5 à 7*.

What immediately stands out is a great fondness for words embedded in two very cinematic films. *À bout de souffle* is brimming with (mostly American) film posters, book titles, newspapers, poems, neon signs, even down to the private jokes (the girl in the street offering Michel a copy of

Cahiers du cinéma, for instance). Godard is simply interested in texts, not images/films on the one hand and words/books on the other. He does not differentiate between literature and cinema. *Cléo* is also teeming with words, either spoken or written (shop names, the title cards in the film-within-the-film, one notable film poster of Luis Buñuel's surrealist *Un chien andalou/An Andalusian Dog*, 1929, opposite Cléo's building – which may well be an homage – street signs, bus stops – the very poetic 'Verlaine' in particular – and so on). Some even criticised the film for being too verbose – Varda herself facetiously remarks that 'in the word "bavardage" [chatter], there's "Varda".'[49] Varda had earlier described *La Pointe courte* as 'a film to be read'.[50] In her writing, interviews and *cinécriture*, Varda is very inventive, constantly playing with words and delving into their deeper meanings (*Les Glaneurs et la glaneuse* is a case in point, where she examines the meanings of the verb 'to glean'). However, whereas Varda soon left overt 'literariness' behind (the chapter titles, for instance, which she used only in *L'Opéra-Mouffe* and *Cléo*, but abandoned thereafter), Godard continued in this vein and has never given up the written word: *Histoire(s) du cinéma* (1988–1998) is fairly brimming with words.

Varda and Godard's second shared concern was topicality. *À bout de souffle* was topical in the sense that it captured a modern, youthful and energetic Paris. Its narrative strategies borrowed from modernism and the *nouveau roman*, revealing its creative process (real people staring into the camera; Michel addressing the audience). Generically, being a French reworking of 1950s American B-thrillers, *À bout de souffle* is far from socially realist, yet there are a few details that echo France's rapid social changes of the 1960s: the influx of foreigners (particularly Americans) in Paris, increased travel, mass consumerism (Michel's quip that supermarket dresses are much nicer than Dior couture) and a rejection of elitist culture. Yet, as Susan Hayward suggests, 'Varda's topicality is of a very different order. Having first realised the topicality of an issue and the need to translate it into film as a marker of a particular generation or movement, she then proceeds to document that issue in a non-conflictive way. It is in this respect that Varda's films can be seen as non-ideological and yet replete with socio-economic realism.'[51] This is very true: Varda is not a *provocatrice* and her films are more 'subjective documentaries' than Godard's films could ever be. An *auteur* she may be, but her films are not first and foremost 'Vardian' as one would say 'Godardian'; they are not steeped in her personality. Nor are they intended to be controversial. Rather like the word 'cancer', which is uttered only once, 'Algérie' is mentioned only three times.

Many diseases go through phases of high visibility in art, culture and society: syphilis in the eighteenth and nineteenth centuries, tuberculosis in the nineteenth and early twentieth centuries, and HIV/AIDS from the mid-1980s on. The ailment of the 1950s and 1960s was undoubtedly cancer, and still is to a certain extent. What captures the popular imagination is that these diseases are largely *invisible*, at least in their early stages, and because medicine is often ineffective, they are seen as mysterious and insidious. Moreover, they are often perceived as forms of punishment, as Susan Sontag examined in her books, *Illness as Metaphor* (1978) and *AIDS and its Metaphors* (1988). In the former work, Sontag showed how the metaphors and myths surrounding certain illnesses, especially cancer, add greatly to the suffering of patients and often inhibit them from seeking proper treatment. Cancer, she argued, is not a curse nor a punishment, and certainly not an embarrassment. Cléo's attitude towards cancer is one of heightened and obsessive fear, to the point where she believes that uttering the very word will bring her bad luck. Even her doctor does not pronounce it at the end of the film, but synechdochically mentions the treatment, radiation, instead. Sontag explains that '[i]n France and Italy it is still the rule for doctors to communicate a cancer diagnosis to the patient's family but not to the patient; doctors consider that the truth will be intolerable to all but exceptionally mature and intelligent patients. (A leading French oncologist has told me that fewer than a tenth of his patients know they have cancer.)'[52] As Flitterman-Lewis has noted, as soon as Cléo pronounces the word 'cancer' in *Chapter 12*, '[a]s soon as she verbalizes her fears, the freedom and openness of this relationship with Antoine is made possible'.[53] It is interesting that Sontag added a study of AIDS ten years later, thus establishing a parallel between cancer and AIDS and the language used to discuss them, because in the 1980s, Madonna approached Varda about doing an American-style remake of *Cléo de 5 à 7*. Madonna would have played the lead character who is awaiting the result of an AIDS test. However, Madonna was not satisfied with the adaptation of the script in English and the project never came to fruition.[54]

Finally, to return to the Varda–Godard comparison, both are very eclectic in their citations of other art forms. Whereas Truffaut's early films were more instinctive and autobiographical, Godard's cinema was highly erudite and his points of reference were by no means restricted to the past offerings of the *Cinémathèque*. Similarly, as previously mentioned in the genesis of *Cléo*, Varda displayed a wide array of inspirational sources: painting, photography, music, literature, poetry, and possibly also film, but to a much lesser degree than Godard. This intellectual eclecticism is also present in Alain Resnais's cinema, though Varda's playfulness is much closer in spirit to the *Cahiers* group. The 'private joke' of the New Wave actors in the film-within-the-film, which also draws on early cinema, is unimaginable in Resnais's early films.

As Sandy Flitterman-Lewis has argued in her excellent and thorough chapter on *Cléo de 5 à 7* in the context of the New Wave, there is no doubt that the film falls very squarely into the New Wave category, even though it is less celebrated than more iconic films such as *Les Quatre cents coups* or *À bout de souffle*. As far as New Wave 'criteria' go, *Cléo* ticks all the boxes: it was made before 1963, which is often cited as the year of the demise, or at least the beginning of the end, of the New Wave; it was low-budget and 'amateurish', i.e. not slick and polished like Tradition of Quality films, and consequently, more free in its subject matter and style; it was an *auteur* film in the sense that it bore the director's control and stamp – it was written by Varda herself; it had recourse to little-known actors and some non-professionals; it referred to other New Wave film-makers and actors via the in-joke of the short burlesque film; it did reasonably well at the box office, though not as well as other New Wave films or competing Tradition of Quality films;[55] it was shot on location in Paris; and last but not least, *Cléo* had that youthfulness and energy so characteristic of New Wave films and which was refreshing after a diet of ossified 'quality' films.

Yet, as mentioned earlier, Varda did not have an agenda like her peers, she was not consciously working against the *cinéma du papa*. It just so happened that she had the determination to make films without the necessary wherewithal or experience, something that all New Wave film-makers had in common, give or take a few family inheritances or windfalls (Chabrol and Truffaut, for instance, who respectively married into money and big distribution companies).[56]

Historical contexts: the backdrop of the Algerian war

During the making of *Cléo de 5 à 7*, the Algerian war was still raging. It had started on 1 November 1954 and would end with the Évian Agreement of 18 March 1962, which led to Algeria becoming independent on 3 July 1962. However, French cinema could not refer explicitly to the conflict until 1963. From 1954 to 1962, many French intellectuals, including New Wave film-makers, were strongly opposed to the Algerian war. In 1961, many (400 of them to be precise) signed the 'Manifesto of the 121' (thus called because it started out with 121 signees but soon swelled to 400), which urged French soldiers to desert rather than fight. This was intended to damage some film-makers' careers because the government forbade anyone to publicise the names of those who had signed the manifesto, but the state-owned media also prohibited any radio or TV appearances by those signees, thus demolishing their attempts at promotion of newly released films.[57] Some films were banned outright, such as, notoriously, Godard's *Le Petit soldat/The Little Soldier* (completed in 1960 but released after the end of the conflict in 1963, though with cuts to the soundtrack). *Le Petit soldat* was far too explicit in its depiction of how the FLN (Front de Libération National), who were pro-desertion and opposed to the war, and the OAS (Organisation Armée Secrète) French commandos practised torture and espionage. In 1960, the film was deemed to be pro-FLN, yet when it was released, it was accused of being pro-OAS. This had a lot to do with the film's own ambiguity; contrary to Godard's 'leftist' image, he only showed the FLN practising torture. Before 1963, only oblique *allusions* to Algeria were acceptable; after 1963, films could be more explicit or build their narratives around the war (Alain Resnais's *Muriel ou le temps d'un retour/Muriel or the Time of Return*, 1963, which mentions torture, and Jacques Demy's *Les Parapluies de Cherbourg*, 1964, which beautifully showed how the war also destroyed the lives of those who remained in France). Films still couldn't show what had actually happened in Algeria, but they could show how it affected lives in France. This is still an uncomfortable subject in French cinema or television, even to this day, though there have been a few incursions such as Brigitte Rouän's *Outremer/Overseas* (1990) and Bertrand Tavernier's *La Guerre sans nom/The Undeclared War* (1992).

Unlike Truffaut and Resnais, but like Godard, Varda did not sign the manifesto, yet she showed her discontent through her films. She was admittedly less ostentatious and reckless than Godard, but she did refer to Algeria, implicitly rather than explicitly. Before *Cléo de 5 à 7*, she had already broached the topic by choosing to pan across a wall in *L'Opéra-Mouffe* on which an anti-war graffiti is clearly scrawled in big capital letters: 'PAIX. ALGÉRIE FRANÇAISE [with 'française' crossed out]' ('Peace. French Algeria [with 'French' crossed out]'). In *Cléo*, however, she took this further by referring to Algeria three times: on the real-life news bulletin on the radio during the first taxi ride, through a snippet of conversation in the Dôme café ('It's stupid what's going on in Algeria. Damned politicians. We never quite know what's really going on') and through Cléo's encounter with the soldier, Antoine.

In *Chapter 4*, in the second half of the taxi ride, the female taxi driver switches the radio back on. At first, we hear an advert for a whisky shampoo, then an announcement that it is twenty past five, and time for the news. This bulletin really existed and had been broadcast by Europe 1 on 21 June 1961. As the taxi advances down the rue de Condé, a male newsreader begins with an item about Muslim rioting near Djidjelli in the Constantine region. 'The casualty figures for the last three days: 20 dead and 60 wounded.' He then continues with a second item connected to Algeria: 'In Paris, before a military tribunal, Commander Robin, a rebel in the Algerian uprising of the 22nd April, has been sentenced to six years in prison.' Georges Robin had been involved in the Algiers putsch of 22 April 1961 led by four retired generals who were rebelling against General de Gaulle's policies on Algeria, which they deemed to be too pro-independence. The newsreader's tone is neutral and there are no indications of any bias, be it anti- or pro-independence. The newsreader then moves on to farmers' demonstrations in France, a rather jolly item about Khrushchev and a dog, a fatal sewer accident, the Fontainebleau Museum closed to the public, Édith Piaf's recovery after her operation and Robert Platten crossing the Channel on a four-poster bed. The two items on Algeria take up just one minute and three seconds, the time it takes the taxi to turn the corner of the rue de Condé and the rue de Vaugirard and continue past the Sénat. It is clear that events like these are a daily occurrence, yet they are still a priority above the rest of the news. It is a brief moment, but stands out from the other, generally more light-hearted, news items, both in the radio broadcast and in the film. There are three reasons for this: firstly, none of the three occupants of the taxi speak during these two items. Cléo and Angèle exchange a few words later, after the mention of Khrushchev's gift of a dog to the White House. Secondly, the scenery may vary, but the camera angle doesn't; within one long take, it is positioned to the driver's right so that we can see the road ahead, without being visually distracted by cutaways. Thirdly, and retrospectively, it is shocking to us now (but it may have been shocking also to contemporary audiences) to hear a *genuine* (and this is corroborated at the end by the mention of 'tomorrow, the 22nd of June') reference to events in Algeria at a specific time. Paris is sunny, beautiful, normal, with people going to work, getting on and off buses, crossing roads, art students are messing around, yet hundreds of miles away, people are dying every day. It is the contrast with the smooth and pleasant taxi ride that makes this detail so poignant.

The ubiquity of Algeria is further demonstrated in *Chapter 8* when we overhear a Dôme patron saying, 'C'est stupide, ces événements d'Algérie. Foutus politiques. On ne sait plus exactement où on en est' ('It's stupid what's going on in Algeria. Damned politicians. We never quite know what's really going on') and in *Chapter 11* when Cléo meets Antoine, who is on leave. 'I'm half in uniform,' he says, 'I leave tonight. I've had three weeks. I've done nothing, it's too short.' The word 'Algeria' hasn't yet been pronounced, yet it is obvious that that is where he is fighting. He does mention it later, on the bench, when Cléo tells him she's scared of everything. 'In Algeria, you'd be scared all the time, then,' he says, to which she replies a hushed, 'how dreadful!' Antoine never goes into detail about the situation in Algeria, but despite his jollity, he does express his discontent, and particularly, the feeling that his life may be wasted for nothing. This feeling was shared by many French people at the time, either because they were in favour of Algeria's independence and the withdrawal of French troops, or, like the rebelling generals of the Algiers putsch, because they felt that it was wrong for lives, whether French or Algerian, to have been wasted in vain if Algeria was not to be retained as one of France's colonies. Antoine does not bring politics into it; we do not know which side he is on, if any. Nor is the possibility of desertion ever evoked. National conscription was still compulsory at that time, so young men could not opt out. But Antoine is certainly acutely aware of the futility of war, that surely all of this could have been settled in a less ruthless and bloody way (the Algerian war caused over a million deaths in total): 'What upsets me is to die for nothing. Giving your life up for war is a bit sad. I'd rather have given it up for a woman, to have died from love.'

I hope to have shown that despite Varda's unorthodox beginnings as a film-maker, *Cléo de 5 à 7* bears virtually all the hallmarks of a New Wave film through its production values, social and historical contexts and filmic style. In the following chapter, I propose to examine the film's stylistic and thematic content in greater detail, as well as its unique narrative structure.

Notes

1   Varda claims that her mother named her Arlette because she had been conceived in Arles. Varda disliked the diminutive nature and excessive femininity ('-ette') of the name and changed it to the stronger, Greek name of Agnès in her late teens. Varda, Agnès, *Varda par Agnès* (Paris: Cahiers du cinéma, 1994), p. 10.
2   Varda: *Agnès*, p. 25.
3   Varda: *Agnès*, p. 13.
4   Lejeune, Paule, *Le Cinéma des femmes: 105 femmes cinéastes d'expression française (France, Belgique, Suisse) 1895–1987* (Paris: L'Atlas/L'Herminier, 1987), p. 213.
5   Varda: *Agnès*, pp. 39–47.
6   Varda: *Agnès*, p. 38.
7   Varda: *Agnès*, p. 39.
8   Neupert, Richard, *A History of the French New Wave* (Madison: University of Wisconsin Press, 2002), p. 57.
9   Neupert: *A History of the French New Wave*, p. 61.
10   Levitin, Jacqueline, 'Mother of the New Wave: an interview with Agnès Varda', *Women and Film* 1.5–6 (1974), p. 63.
11   Fieschi, Jean-André, and Claude Ollier, 'La Grâce laïque', *Cahiers du cinéma* 165, April 1965, p. 47.
12   Levitin: 'Mother of the New Wave', p. 63.

13   Varda: *Agnès*, p. 40.
14   On a purely anecdotal note, Georges de Beauregard appears in a very brief cameo in *Cléo* as the ambulance/hearse driver in the short burlesque film. Varda had presumably switched from Pierre Braunberger to de Beauregard because de Beauregard had produced Jacques Demy's first feature, *Lola*, in 1961. According to Varda, de Beauregard earned so much from producing Godard's *À bout de souffle* that he asked Godard if he had any friends interested in making movies, so Godard sent him Demy. And Demy introduced him to Varda. (Neupert: *A History of the French New Wave*, p. 42.)
15   Varda: *Agnès*, p. 48.
16   Varda: *Agnès*, p. 48.
17   'And if I could make *Cléo* about femininity and fear of death, it is because the girl was beautiful.' Levitin: 'Mother of the New Wave', p. 64.
18   *Cléo de 5 à 7* pressbook for its British release.
19   Pressbook.
20   Douchet, Jean, *French New Wave* (New York: Distributed Art Publishers, 1999), p. 257.
21   Varda: *Agnès*, p. 52.
22   In France, the 'Bibliothèque Rose' is a well-known Hachette imprint of pink hardback children's classics (intended for little girls, hence the colour pink, as opposed to the 'Bibliothèque Verte' for little boys and older girls), including the popular stories written by the Comtesse de Ségur. By that, I think Varda meant that she wanted him to be a clichéd 'fairytale lover'. Quoted in Manceaux, Michèle, 'Reportage: Agnès Varda', *L'Express*, 29 June 1961.
23   Varda: *Cléo de 5 à 7* (Paris: Gallimard, 1962), p. 41.
24   Varda: *Agnès*, p. 56.
25   Frodon, Jean-Michel, *L'Age moderne du cinéma français: De la Nouvelle Vague à nos jours* (Paris: Flammarion, 1995), p. 129.
26   Varda: *Agnès*, p. 31.
27   Varda: *Agnès*, p. 53.
28   Caen, Michel, and Alain Le Bris, 'Entretien avec Jacques Demy', *Cahiers du cinéma*, May 1964, p. 10.
29   Lacassin, Francis and Yolande Wagner, 'Avec Corinne Marchand de 5 à 7', *Cinéma* 62, June 1962, p. 65.
30   This said, there is a five-minute 'slippage' of time at the end of *Chapter 7*, just as Cléo is about to enter the Dôme: a street clock reads 17.50, yet *Chapter 8* announces, '17.45–17.52'. Is the clock fast?
31   Varda quoted in Jean de Baroncelli, '*Cléo de 5 à 7*', *Le Monde*, 23 April 1962.
32   Manceaux, Michèle, 'Cléo de 5 à 7': interview with Agnès Varda, *L'Express*, 29 June 1961.
33   Bogart, Betsy Ann, *Music and Narrative in the French New Wave: The Films of Agnès Varda and Jacques Demy* (Ann Arbor, MI: University Microfilms, 2001), p. 212.
34   Bogart: *Music and Narrative* ..., p. 240.
35   See, for example, the title of Jacqueline Levitin's interview of Varda.
36   Powell, Nicholas, 'Agnès Varda, the alternative voice', *Times*, 31 May 1986.
37   See Siclier, Jacques, *Nouvelle Vague?* (Paris: Éditions du Cerf, 1961), p. 58, or Vincendeau, Ginette in Annette Kuhn and Susannah Radstone (eds), *The Women's Companion to International Film* (Berkeley: University of California Press, 1994), p. 411.

38 One director of photography, Quinto Albicocco, unused to working with female directors, insisted on calling her 'Ginette' during the making of *Ô saisons, ô châteaux*, convinced that all female personnel were (or should be) called 'Ginette'. She had to put him straight and they became good friends after that. Varda: *Agnès*, p. 75.

39 Flitterman-Lewis, Sandy, *To Desire Differently: Feminism and the French Cinema* (expanded edn) (New York: Columbia University Press, 1996), p. 258.

40 Harkness, John, 'Agnès Varda: improvised inspiration', *Now*, 19–25 June 1986, quoted in Flitterman-Lewis, *To Desire Differently: Feminism and the French Cinema* p. 258.

41 Varda: *Agnès*, p. 59.

42 Monaco, James, *The New Wave* (New York: Oxford University Press, 1976).

43 Clouzot, Claire, *Le Cinéma français depuis la nouvelle vague* (Paris: Fernand Nathan-Alliance Française, 1972), p.48.

44 Flitterman-Lewis: *To Desire Differently*, p. 258.

45 Shivas, Mark, '*Cléo de 5 à 7* and Agnès Varda', *Movie* 3, October 1962, p. 35.

46 Chabrol, Claude, *Arts* 658, 19 February 1958, quoted in Siclier: *Nouvelle Vague?*, p. 15.

47 Varda: *Agnès*, pp. 19–20.

48 Levitin: 'Mother of the New Wave', p. 103.

49 Varda: *Agnès*, p. 11. 'Dans le mot "bavardage", il y a "Varda".'

50 Fieschi and Ollier: 'La Grâce laïque,' p. 45. 'Un film à lire.'

51 Hayward, Susan, *French National Cinema* (London: Routledge, 1993), p. 256.

52 Sontag, Susan, *Illness as Metaphor and AIDS and its Metaphors* (London: Penguin Classics, 2002), p. 7.

53 Flitterman-Lewis: *To Desire Differently*, p. 282.

54 Varda: *Agnès*, p. 60.

55 The number of admissions for *Cléo* was 553,545 (263,911 in Paris alone). Compare this to *Les Quatre cents coups*: 3,642,981 (772,707 in Paris). (Figures taken from Simsi, Simon, *Ciné-Passions: Premier guide chiffré du cinéma en France* (Paris: Éditions Dixit, 2000), pp. 34 and 124 respectively.)

56 Marie, Michel, *La Nouvelle Vague: Une école artistique,* (Paris: Nathan Université, 1997) pp. 53–54.

57 Neupert: *A History of the French New Wave*, p. 190.

2 Structure, style and themes

An unusual narrative structure: 13 chapters in 'real' time

Possibly the first thing to strike viewers is that *Cléo de 5 à 7* is narrated in physical, or – theoretically – 'real', time. Ira Konigsberg's definition of physical time is 'the actual duration in which the entire film takes place'.[1] In other words, the time of the narration, or diegesis, that is to say the world of the film, matches the film's running time, also known as the projection time or screen duration, which is usually between 90 and 120 minutes. Film normally creates a dramatic temporality that exceeds the viewing time by hours, days, months, years or even centuries. *Cléo* was by no means the first – or last – film to be shot in 'real' time. Celebrated examples include Alfred Hitchcock's *Rope* (1948), which also attempted to appear to have been shot in one continuous take, Fred Zinnemann's *High Noon* (1952) and more recently, Aleksandr Sokurov's tour-de-force one-take feature-length film, *Russian Ark* (2002), although it in fact charted several centuries of Russian history through St Petersburg's Ermitage collection.[2] However, no film has been as exact as *Cléo* in its matching of narration time and projection time.

Filmic narration can be divided into story and plot. The two are rarely equivalent. To use Bruce Kawin's definition, the story 'is the series of hypothetical events as they "happen" in the time of the fiction or of factual events in history. The plot is the order in which selected story-events are arranged; [...] The story of *Citizen Kane* begins when Kane's mother decides that her son should be raised by a banker, but its plot begins with Kane's death.'[3] Similarly, as David Bordwell has noted in *Narration in the Fiction Film*, 'a film's fabula [the Russian Formalists' term for 'story'] is never materially present on the screen or soundtrack'.[4] In other words, during the unfurling of the plot, we infer certain facts and events that are not shown in the film. In *Cléo de 5 à 7*, for example, we are not shown the Algerian war, which was raging at the time, but it is referred to several times. This said, *Cléo* is remarkable for its resistance to a story. We know very little about Cléo beyond the confines of the 90-minute plot. Where is she from? How did she meet Angèle, José, Bob and Dorothée? When and how did she become a singer? How long has she lived in Paris? In that particular street (since she seems so ignorant of her own neighbourhood, unlike Dorothée)? Last but not least, will she see Antoine again and will she survive cancer? We do know about the war (I will revert to this later) and we do know that Cléo had a biopsy a few days earlier and is awaiting the result that afternoon. We also know that Cléo and Dorothée are quite old friends since Dorothée mentions in *Chapter 9* that she hasn't seen Cléo for a while and evokes the 'good old days' when Cléo wanted to be a singer, Bob a jazz musician while she herself aspired to be a dancer. We also learn that Cléo has recorded three singles, hence her being recognised by the shop assistant at the hatter's in *Chapter 3*. But aside from these details, plot and story are conflated.

Cléo's plot begins in the credits sequence at 17.00 and ends in *Chapter 13* at 18.30. The film's running time is exactly 90 minutes. Thus the physical time is perfectly respected, even if the film's title is inaccurate.[5] This is no doubt because it would have been inelegant to call it *Cléo de 5 heures à 6 heures et demie* and moreover, we would have lost the superb double entendre explained in the previous chapter, namely that a 'cinq à sept' designates the two-hour late afternoon slot when married men meet their mistresses, or more generally an afternoon lovers' tryst.

Films shot in real time can be technically arduous, particularly when it comes to natural lighting and consistency of weather conditions, since shooting a feature-length film will always take much longer than 90 minutes. In the case of *Cléo*, exteriors had to be filmed at the same time of day as in the narration and in identical (i.e. sunny) weather conditions. This is where the three-month delay in shooting from March to June 1961 was so fortuitous. In spring, Varda might have had to endure varied and/or poor weather, whereas in summer, she was blessed with almost totally unadulterated long and sunny days.

Unlike most New Wave films, *Cléo* follows a very traditional, and some might say literary or theatrical, narrative structure. After the five-minute credits sequence, which acts as a sort of prologue, there are 13 chapters averaging six and a half minutes each, with the longest being the final chapter (15 minutes). With uncanny (but certainly not accidental) precision, the end of *Chapter 7*, which features the turning point in the narrative, marks the 45-minute point, exactly midway through the 90-minute running time.

From what I have just described, there appears to be no manipulation of time whatsoever; no ellipses, and no compression or expansion. This would seem extraordinary, an absolute tour de force in filmic terms. Yet, is this really the case? And if so, how does *Cléo* manage to be so compelling, and ultimately quite dramatic? Let us examine the beginning of *Chapter 1* in detail.

I want to analyse only the first 37 seconds, from the moment Cléo leaves the fortune-teller's flat to the moment she reaches the ground floor of the building. This chapter ('Cléo from 17.05–17.08') begins just after the fortune-teller, Madame Irma (Loye Payen), has told her husband (who is reading the newspaper in the toilet) that she saw death and cancer in Cléo's hand.

1. Medium shot of Cléo emerging from the left, from behind a wall, onto the landing. She passes a window on the right and is looking down. Her expression is neutral, perhaps a little pensive. Just before she exits screen left, she looks off-screen right.

2. High-angle POV (point-of-view)[6] medium shot of three women and one man seated in a row in a narrow corridor, facing a window on the right. We assume that they are waiting their turn for the fortune-teller. The last woman looks straight at the camera/Cléo.

3. The camera crosses the 180° line and shows Cléo in medium long shot edging her way past the clients. As she approaches the camera, the first woman in the row stands up and walks away and the other three look up at Cléo as she passes. The camera pans right as Cléo, in profile right, looks down and begins her descent of the stairs. We can hear her footsteps very distinctly on the wooden treads. The music on the theme of 'La Belle P.' begins in tempo with her footsteps. The camera tracks left and tilts down as she descends so that the shot becomes increasingly high-angle.

4. Frontal medium shot of Cléo on the left of the frame going down the stairs against the peeling plaster wall of the stairwell. She looks vacantly off-screen left and down.

5. Frontal medium close-up of a window and in the background, we can see the opposite wall of the courtyard. This is the second POV shot: the camera pans down jerkily, as if moving step by step, before turning abruptly right on the landing.

6. Medium shot of Cléo passing a window and rubbing her neck with her right hand, shot from profile right. She crosses the landing, with the camera panning right, before she looks down to begin her descent of the second flight of stairs. The lighting is darker, indicating her progression into the depths of the stairwell (seemingly lit only by natural daylight).

7. Identical set-up to shot 4. However, it is followed by three very brief close-ups from exactly the same angle (thus breaking the 30° rule). The shots are identical, merely repeated, in time with the beat of the music and Cléo's footsteps (see image on p. 26).

8. Downward POV pan of the peeling plaster wall of the stairwell.

9. Frontal medium long shot of Cléo reaching the bottom of the stairs. This is indicated by the curving line of the bannister on the left ending in a graceful pommel. She is strongly lit from above and behind, again indicating that the bottom of the stairs is darker. Cléo has just descended two flights of stairs in 37 seconds.

First of all, it is entirely plausible, temporally speaking, to descend two floors in 37 seconds. Varda shows us the entire process, there are no ellipses as would be expected in films with a more typical treatment of time. Generally, shots or scenes showing characters going up and down stairs, or in and out of doors, are deemed unnecessary to the audience's understanding of the plot and are consequently omitted. However, there is some possible temporal overlap right at the beginning of the chapter, since Cléo should conceivably have progressed further than the fortune-teller's landing during the 15 seconds when Madame Irma was telling her husband about the card and palm reading. Either Cléo, shaken to tears by the verdict, stood for a few seconds outside the door so as to regain her composure, or she may have been listening at the door! Secondly, there is the curious repetition of the close-up of Cléo's face in shot 7. In effect, there are four shots within this shot, in rapid succession, and in tempo with the music and her footsteps. Is it merely playful and jazzy? It is the only shot repetition in the whole film and constitutes a minor enigma. But what I hope has transpired from my breakdown of the first 9 shots is the amount of shots from Cléo's point of view: three! One-third of this scene is shown through her eyes. It would therefore follow that the sound (the music in rhythm with her footsteps, or possibly the other way round) suggests her aural point of view, and the thrice repeated close-up, although not a POV shot, may suggest her perception of time *expanding* at this precise moment. Her gaze is pensive, she appears deep in thought, as if she were mulling over the fortune-teller's words (and ominous silence after reading her palm). Therefore, even though temporally the scene appears very objective, Varda has already inserted a brief moment of *subjective* perception that aligns us with Cléo from the outset.

Aside from the two (possible) exceptions mentioned above, there are a few other manipulations of time: when Cléo changes behind the black curtain in *Chapter 7*; the black screen lasts just two seconds when Cléo would surely

have taken a little longer to don her black dress and shoes. And when Dorothée
and Cléo are in the car after picking up Raoul's film from Montparnasse
station, the film is speeded up a little. In terms of spatial continuity, Cléo is
constantly present on-screen, except for the brief 15 seconds at the end of the
credits sequence when the camera lags behind with the fortune-teller, and a
longer moment in *Chapter 6* (1 minute 14 seconds) when the camera stays
with Bob and Plumitif as they dress up as 'quacks' to amuse Cléo. What about
the short burlesque film (which lasts 2 minutes and 51 seconds)? Cléo is
admittedly 'off-screen' since she is watching it, but the film does not stand
alone. We are aware that she is watching it, and reacting to it (though it is only
at the end of the film that we hear Cléo and Dorothée laughing). It is closely
associated with her. The same could be said for the intriguing 'flashbacks', or
rather 'flashes', that occur during her walk from the Dôme café in *Chapter 8*.
These flashes – very brief and static shots disconnected from her walk and its
environment (builders, old ladies carrying shopping, etc.) – combine familiar
faces from her life, total strangers and physical objects. This is a complex and
pivotal sequence, which deserves to be examined in greater detail, and which
I propose to do later. There are ten flashes in the following order: the frog-
swallowing busker; the man in the café; the fortune-teller; an old man in the
street; a man sitting on a bench reading a paper; Bob posing on a chair; an
eighteenth-century clock (which reads 3.35) with a toy monkey draped over
it; Cléo's lover posing on her bed; Angèle posing on the divan; the top left-

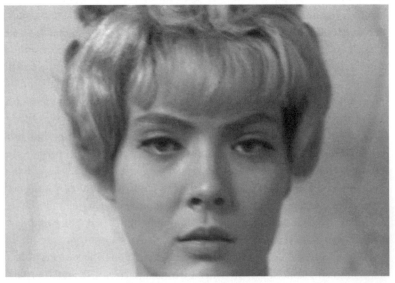

Cléo deep in thought (5.09).

hand corner of Cléo's dressing table mirror, complete with her discarded wig. Although spatially disconnected, these brief shots are all temporally connected through the continuous soundtrack of Cléo's footsteps. The sounds of the street, however, are superseded by the sound of a ticking clock or a metronome, which covers the last four flashes. We are now in the realm of aural, as well as visual, subjectivity. Consequently, it would arguably be incorrect to identify a temporal ellipsis, or rather expansion, here. While these images are playing in her mind and on-screen, the story time has not stopped, her footsteps have slowed down during the last three shots, but she is still walking down that street. In other words, there is no hint of expansion by *insertion*, where story time would be expanded by a 'padding' of foreign matter, and the story time would be momentarily interrupted.[7] When we revert to Cléo walking, she has progressed down the street (the rue Delambre), the shop windows are different, the people are different to the ones previously seen, and she then emerges onto a funeral procession on the Boulevard Edgar Quinet. The same could be said of the very brief inserts of close-ups of death masks during the taxi ride down the rue Guénégaud in *Chapter 3*.

There are other ellipses, but these are so subtle as to be missed altogether (as I did until they were pointed out to me). Certain actions are speeded up, though by no means implausibly: Angèle boils the kettle rather fast in *Chapter 5*; Cléo quickly arrives at Dorothée's sculpture school in *Chapter 8*, though she is admittedly running part of the way to escape the sight of the busker skewering his arm; the wait in Dorothée's car in *Chapter 9* is perhaps not as long as it should be – surely it would take Dorothée a little longer to collect the film?; the two final taxi rides (from the Cinéma Delambre via the Place Denfert before dropping off Dorothée, and then into the Parc Montsouris) seem very smooth and quick; and last but not least, the bus ride, which covers a sizeable chunk of the Left Bank (from the park via Place d'Italie to the northern end of the Boulevard de l'Hôpital – that's most of the 13th arrondissement), must contain some ellipses. This said, car and bus journeys were admittedly quicker in the 1960s: there was less traffic and thus fewer red lights; the old-style buses with platforms at the back were, like the London Routemasters, quicker to board and alight. Nevertheless, it is fair to say that Varda most probably cut a few temporal corners here and there, though without ever losing the appearance of 'quotidianness' and spatio-temporal realism (unlike Godard's hatchet-like chopping up of *À bout de souffle...*). Unlike other New Wave films, Varda did not go in for 'dead time' (cf. the 30-minute hotel bedroom sequence in *À bout de souffle*). Her characters do not hang around or stand still. Even in her apartment, Cléo is busy, and as a result, these 90 minutes of an 'ordinary day' in her life seem quite packed.

Although Varda does not mention it anywhere, the structure of 13 chapters with its mid-point being *Chapter 7* is strongly reminiscent of a celebrated French realist novel by Émile Zola, *L'Assommoir* (1876), which also has 13 chapters and a seventh watershed chapter. *L'Assommoir*, the sixth volume of the Rougon-Macquart series, recounts the life of a woman, Gervaise, in a working-class area of late nineteenth-century Paris. She runs a successful laundry business but her husband, unable to work after a roofing accident, turns to alcohol and she later also succumbs to absinthe and dies homeless and in poverty. Gervaise is as superstitious as Cléo (in *Chapter 7*, in fact, she worries about having 13 guests to her party and so invites a poor neighbour off the street to make up 14 people), and so a total of 13 chapters seems very apposite, particularly since Gervaise dies a horrible and lonely death in the final chapter. Admittedly, the plots of *L'Assommoir* and *Cléo* are very different, but the linear narrative structure contained in the same number of chapters with the mid-point signalling a watershed in the characters' fates is noteworthy.

There is certainly something very literary about this structure. First of all, it is unusual to have chapters in films, and even more so chapter titles. Admittedly, Godard used them in *Vivre sa vie* (1962) and Quentin Tarantino is fond of them (*Pulp Fiction*, 1994; *Kill Bill Volumes 1 and 2*, 2004), but that is the exception rather than the rule. Secondly, although *Cléo* abides by Nicolas Boileau's famous seventeenth-century rule of French classical theatre, which advocated unity of place, time and action,[8] the film does not follow the three-act structure that is the norm in theatre, French or otherwise, and that has been adopted to a large extent by mainstream (especially Hollywood) cinema. Instead of the typical disruption – complication – resolution/closure pattern, *Cléo* has a binary structure that is articulated around the mid-point when Cléo leaves her flat after the rehearsal.

As mentioned in Chapter One, Varda did not set out, like Godard for example, or more experimental contemporary film-makers such as Isidore Isou, to overthrow the rules of filmic narration.[9] This is not counter-cinema, but it is not mainstream cinema either. In terms of its narrative codes, *Cléo de 5 à 7* follows elements of a classic narrative structure, but with interesting variations. Let us examine these more closely.

To what extent then does *Cléo* follow what Noël Burch termed the institutional mode of representation (IMR), or what we tend to call the (Western) classic narrative structure, namely the structure that dominates classical Hollywood cinema?[10] First of all, in the classic model, events in the story are organised around a basic dialectic of enigma and resolution. This can also be called disruption.[11] There is indeed an event in *Cléo*'s story that pre-dates the beginning of the plot, and certainly disrupts a pre-existing equilibrium, and that is Cléo's medical test, whose result she anxiously awaits. However, the actual diagnosis and prognosis are not what really matter. When *Cléo* was first released in 1962, Varda handed out short questionnaires to the audience to discover their reactions to the film. One member of the audience was a young Serge Daney, who would go on to become a well-known film critic for *Cahiers du cinéma*. Varda published his questionnaire in her *Varda par Agnès* book.[12] To the question 'Will Cléo die?', Daney replied: 'AUCUNE IMPORTANCE' (unimportant) in capitals. Daney was correct; Cléo's possible death or recovery is the film's MacGuffin. We may recall that this was a term devised by Alfred Hitchcock to describe a plot device that moved the action forward and created dramatic effect. Whereas the characters may care a great deal about a MacGuffin, the audience care very little about it.[13] However, there may be an alternative enigma and resolution: Cléo's existential angst at the beginning and her journey towards serenity at the end.

As mentioned previously, *Cléo de 5 à 7* has the ultimate linear structure with remarkably few instances of spatial and temporal manipulation. There is spatial verisimilitude; we know where we are at all times, there is no discontinuity between one location and another, we can follow Cléo's itinerary on a map (in fact published with the screenplay).[14] However, this often overlaps in outdoor scenes with documentary-style realism, which is not the same thing as verisimilitude and which may in fact detract from our involvement in the film.

This, as well as other details, makes it immediately obvious that this is no classical Hollywood narrative, but very much a European art movie. The extreme linearity of the narrative is quite Brechtian and leads to moments of spectator distanciation and alienation (or *Verfremdungseffekt*), as indeed do the chapter headings. Rather than lose track of time – an ideal in Hollywood cinema – we are constantly reminded of it. As Varda put it, 'The time shown every ten minutes implies real time juxtaposing the time of the film and this creates a distance towards the characters.'[15] Spatially, there are a number of violations of continuity editing rules (breaking the 180° rule, for example), though these are by no means disruptive or puzzling. For Jill Forbes, *Cléo*'s distinctive time-frame strongly evokes 'women's time', namely time that is spent waiting or doing dull, household chores (as in Chantal Akerman's *Jeanne Dielman, 23 Quai du Commerce, 1080 Bruxelles*, 1976). Even though *Cléo* is unique among women's films in its conflation of narration time and screen duration, it is very different to other 'real time' films, which are geared towards a more masculine and eventful 'deadline' (getting caught, or not, in *Rope*; Kane (Gary Cooper) facing the man he sent to prison in *High*

Noon), which renders the narrative more exciting and suspenseful (the murder and the party in *Rope*; Kane's wedding, his decision to stay in town and face his nemesis alone in *High Noon*). Even though we do have a deadline in *Cléo* (the rather anticlimactic diagnosis) and the film's events are momentous as part of an 'ordinary' life, it is largely a film about waiting, and it is impossible to describe it as an exciting, nail-biting wait. This said, *Cléo* is nevertheless very different to *Jeanne Dielman*: Cléo is hardly doing dull, repetitive household chores, her life is more exciting and more 'extra-ordinary', and those particular 90 minutes are more eventful than Jeanne's empty three days or so conveyed in three hours and 20 minutes (the murder excepted).

Varda obviously prefers to focus on her characters' subjective states rather than a classic enigma resolution trajectory. Though again, this is by no means challenging or disconcerting in the way that the portrayal of subjective states tends to be, for instance in Alain Resnais's *L'Année dernière à Marienbad/Last Year At Marienbad* (1961). Nevertheless, when characters discuss time (which is often), they all dwell on different aspects. Cléo cannot bear to think about the future and is evasive when José suggests they go out on Friday night. 'If all goes well,' she cautiously responds. José, on the other hand, as Elizabeth Anthony has noted, is unable to live in the present; he is either evoking the past ('There's always something the matter with you') or the future (his meetings, outings, holidays). On the other hand, neither Cléo nor Antoine wears a watch, and Antoine is certainly not a slave to time like José: 'It appears that Antoine copes with his fear of dying for no reason in Algeria by stretching out the present and observing the life around him.'[16] Which is something Cléo emulates: 'We have all the time in the world,' she says in the final chapter, despite Antoine's train leaving in an hour and a half. The omnipresence of time highlights the characters' subjective states, something that is paramount to Varda.

A 'subjective documentary': focalisation, character interiority and realism

For Agnès Varda, there is no such thing as an objective documentary.[17] *Cléo de 5 à 7* is admittedly a fiction film and not a documentary, but Varda's intention was to show a realistic Paris seen through the eyes of a woman who is racked by the fear of death. However, the film is not only concerned with Cléo's subjectivity, but that of other characters as well.

Cléo de 5 à 7 is narrated largely in variable internal focalisation (alternating with some external focalisation). This means that the camera closely follows, or is aligned with, a specific character, or several characters; in addition, we are often made aware that a character's subjectivity is being explored through the following filmic strategies: internal monologue (where the character is on-screen but his/her lips are not moving, which is distinct from voiceover, where the character is off-screen), so that we know what they are thinking; POV shots and subjective tracking shots, so that we know what they are seeing; and occasionally, aural POV, so that we know what they are hearing.

Visual and aural point of view is ubiquitous in the film but tends to be confined to Cléo and Angèle. As mentioned earlier, Cléo is granted visual and aural point of view from the outset in *Chapter 1*. *Chapter 2* contains three dual POV shots (i.e. from both women's or either woman's perspective) of the hats in the hatter's window display. We hear Angèle's interior monologue but also Cléo's aural POV of the rowing couple in the café. In *Chapter 3*, we hear Cléo's interior monologue at the hatter's and see Cléo's POV of the road ahead in the taxi and also the African masks. In *Chapter 4*, we switch back to Angèle's interior monologue (about the Beaux Arts students), but are also privy to her very probable aural POV of the taxi driver's story about being attacked, as Cléo is leaning out of the window. However, it is clearly Cléo's visual POV as the taxi driver switches the radio back on. Strangely, POV shots are absent in *Chapters 5* or *6* ('Bob'); there is certainly nothing from Bob's POV, despite the chapter heading. *Chapter 7* features Cléo's interior monologue in front of the Chinese restaurant mirror and several POV shots of the frog-eating busker. *Chapter 8* is by far the most complex chapter in terms of Cléo's subjectivity: it has a subjective tracking shot in the Dôme, accompanied by several POV shots of the patrons. The snippets of conversation are obviously from Cléo's aural POV, particularly the one about models, which spurs her to visit Dorothée. We are shown Cléo's flashbacks and the soundtrack is clearly intended to be subjective with the exaggerated pitch of her footsteps and the sound of a ticking clock or a metronome. Finally, a subjective tracking shot leads us into the sculptor's studio. In *Chapter 9*, Cléo's POV dominates again (despite being entitled 'Dorothée') when Dorothée briefly leaves her at Montparnasse and instructs her to count the sailors' pompoms. Though there are no point/glance shots to confirm that these people are seen from Cléo's point of view, the ensuing dialogue (Cléo telling Dorothée how many pompoms and nuns she has seen) confirms this to be the case. In *Chapter 10*, we have the potential triple POV (Cléo, Dorothée, Raoul) of the silent film. *Chapter 11* contains POV shots mostly from Cléo's perspective (for instance of the observatory in the park), but some POV shots in the early part may be dual with Dorothée (shots of the road ahead through the taxi windscreen, for example). However, all the aural POVs are very clearly Cléo's: the non-diegetic themes on 'La Belle P.' and 'Un Cri d'Amour' as Dorothée climbs the stairs seem to be a dramatisation, a mental soundtrack of what she sees of the latter. *Chapter 12* ('Antoine') has no POV shots at all. Finally, *Chapter 13* ('Cléo et Antoine') contains several dual POV shots of the street from the bus, and a possible dual aural POV (since neither character speaks at the time) of the women talking about the baby in the incubator. The off-screen accented voice of a woman telling a man that every day she visits a new arrondissement may also be dual. The shot of the pregnant woman walking past the funeral home ('Pompes Funèbres') could also be dual, but is more probably Cléo's POV since she is more likely to notice the uncanny birth/death contrast than Antoine. What all this reveals is that Cléo's point of view certainly dominates in the film, but is scattered throughout, with a peak in *Chapter 8*. In the final chapter, she is still observing the world, but her gaze is no longer solitary since it is accompanied by Antoine's.

Each of the 13 chapter titles bears the name of a character, or in some cases, of more than one character (*Chapters 8* – 'Quelques autres' ('Some others') – and *13* – 'Cléo et Antoine'). The title leads us to believe that a chapter is *about* that particular character, but in fact, Varda intended it to show that the events are filtered through that character's subjectivity: '[…] the chapters bear people's names, they colour the narrative, or rather the angle from which Cléo is portrayed.'[18] Each character's perception is different, and to convey this, Varda uses different camera techniques, which does not necessarily mean POV shots. For instance, Angèle's chapters (*2* and *4*) are more static and realist. There is something very down-to-earth and commonsensical about Angèle, despite her ridiculous superstiousness. Her chapters are shot accordingly using wide-angle lenses, which give more definition and seem more grounded. They contrast strongly with Cléo's chapters, which use long-focus lenses that soften the image and slow down the action. As Ira Konigsberg explains, '[…] because long-focus lenses diminish depth and keep the size of objects in different distant planes unnaturally large, a character moving toward or away from the camera will seem to do so with exaggerated slowness.'[19] In addition, Varda chose to use very sinuous and voluptuous camera movements in Cléo's chapters, rendering them not only beautiful and graceful, but also ethereal and dreamlike. Hat shopping (*Chapter 3*) and receiving her lover (*Chapter 5*) seem exceptional and other-wordly events, even though they are probably regular occurrences. In Cléo's chapters, we are aware of the camera, we are conscious of a *mise-en-scène*; Cléo lives her life as if she were in a movie, as if she were acting. As Varda explained in the script, 'When Cléo "imagines herself", she sees herself as being more beautiful than she

Hat shopping: an other-worldly event (12:18).

Receiving José: an other-worldly event (24:36).

already is, more blonde, more *fatale* and less funny; she sees herself as she thinks others like to see her.'[20] Compare this to Dorothée's and Raoul's chapters (*9* and *10*), which are straightforward because, as Varda expressed in the script, 'we mustn't notice the camera'.[21] Finally, there is Bob's chapter (*6*), which is playful and uses a lot of camera movement and a handheld camera style. Varda wanted it filmed 'any old how'[22] to convey Bob's natural and spontaneous rhythm, but also his brusqueness and tactlessness. Antoine's chapter (*12*) is shot in one long take (3 minutes and 8 seconds), 'like a deep breath'.[23] José, Cléo's lover, is so insignificant and fleeting during that hour and a half that he does not even warrant a chapter to himself...

However, nothing is as straightforward as Varda makes out. First of all, I doubt many spectators would consciously notice the lens changes or variations in the *mise-en-scène*, let alone that they reflect changes in characters' perception, though most would notice the interior monologue and POV shots as a clear indicator of shifts in focalisation. One of the film's greatest admirers, Roger Tailleur, admitted that he would not have guessed the meaning of the chapter headings if he hadn't read Varda's foreword to the script.[24] Secondly, other subjectivities intrude in chapters that should in theory focus on just one. A good example of this is *Chapter 2*, entitled 'Angèle'. Cléo's dreamy and narcissistic *Chapter 1* ends as she enters the 'Ça va, ça vient' café looking for Angèle. Having found her, she succumbs to a melodramatic outburst, turning to face a large café mirror that takes up an entire wall. The image is in soft focus (meaning that the background is indistinct) and grainy, giving off a quasi-halo effect on Cléo's blonde hair. Cut to a medium close-up of Angèle facing the camera, with Cléo still partly visible, kneeling on the seat next to her. The chapter title appears. Both women are facing in opposite directions, since Cléo is crying into the mirror, and Angèle is patiently waiting for her to calm down. The image is now sharply focused, with the background (as seen in the mirror, that is) very clear and high-contrast. This highlights Angèle's black hair and strict jacket collar, reflecting her no-nonsense attitude to Cléo's childish whining. Angèle looks off-screen right, and her interior monologue begins, with her facial expression registering resignation and a slightly patronising indulgence, as if she were humouring a toddler's tantrum: 'Such a drama queen. She could be happy but needs to be looked after. She's a child.' Cut to a medium long shot as she turns to comfort Cléo, calling her both deferentially 'Madame' and maternally, 'ma petite fille' ('my little girl'). What follows, however, is a remarkable shift in interiority. After this insight into Angèle's thoughts, Cléo's subjectivity will dominate, though without any need for internal monologue, POV shots or a change in lens.

Cléo's hysterical whimpering attracts the attention of the café owner and a waiter. She cheers up after she orders a coffee, and while she drinks it, Angèle tells the owner a rather long-winded anecdote about a dying Causses farmer who decided to go round the world and whose illness subsequently disappeared. While Angèle is recounting her tale, a cut removes her off-screen, though we can still hear her. The shot frames Cléo head-on in medium shot on the extreme left of the screen sitting against the mirrored wall. The wall ends by her left arm and the right of the screen reveals another room in the café in deep focus. Sitting nearest Cléo at a table are a couple. Their conversation, although hushed, dominates Angèle's voice on the soundtrack. Cléo's expression and gaze (she glances over her left shoulder several times) indicate that she is paying close attention to their argument. The man wants to stay the night at the woman's flat, but she refuses, perhaps because she is ashamed of him. At one point, we overhear Angèle asking 'Are you listening to me?', possibly because the off-screen café owner is also distracted by the couple. The man abruptly gets up and leaves screen left with Cléo's gaze following him. Cut to a long shot of the café's front room with Angèle and Cléo in the centre.

This shot cannot possibly be filtered through Angèle's subjectivity. She cannot see or hear the couple while she is rambling on, and the framing of Cléo and the couple, with the woman in the centre, makes it plain that this is heard (though not really seen) from Cléo's perspective. The fact that the

Melodramatic narcissism: crying in soft focus.

A shift in focalisation through editing (9:10).

couple's words are quite distinct and muffle Angèle's story is an accurate rendering of Cléo's aural selectivity: a public tiff holds far more interest than a story she may have heard many times before. Finally, this scene is crucial at showing that Cléo has begun to observe the world well before *Chapter 7*. She is no longer snivelling in self-pity but is composed and turned towards the outside world and its problems. Thus Cléo's perspective dominates this chapter but it also dominates much of the film, particularly *Chapter 8*, 'Quelques autres', which is supposedly others' views of Cléo and yet turns into an exploration of her visual and aural POV (see the *flâneur* section for a more detailed analysis of this chapter).

Claudia Gorbman, in her excellent essay on the score in *Cléo de 5 à 7*, has identified two musical themes in the film.[25] They are both based on Cléo's songs, 'La Belle P.' (the P stands for 'putain', or 'whore') and 'Un Cri d'Amour'. Gorbman argues that when heard non-diegetically, these themes are subjective and convey Cléo's state of mind. In *Chapter 1*, when Cléo has left the fortune-teller's apartment, the theme of 'La Belle P.' accompanies her footsteps down the stairs and the three repeated jump cuts of Cléo's face are edited in tempo with the music, as if this were the soundtrack of Cléo's mind. This is not the actual song 'La Belle P.' (which we will hear twice diegetically, in the taxi in *Chapter 4*, and on the Dôme café jukebox) but a theme arranged differently. Later, as Cléo steps out into the rue de Rivoli, the arrangement is expressive of Cléo's (self-)perception. As Gorbman details, '[…] the arrangement of ["La Belle P."] in *Chapter 1* is slow, romanticized, played legato by a string ensemble.' It occurs just after Cléo's narcissistic moment with the foyer mirror (see image on p. 46). 'Since Cléo sees herself as an aesthetic object, the convention of a beautiful scene has dictated the presence of beautiful music to enhance it.'[26] Conversely, the theme that dominates the second half of the film is a variation on the song that causes her breakdown in *Chapter 7*: 'Un Cri d'Amour'. Both in terms of its melody (in a minor key) and its lyrics (about death, morbidity, loneliness and absence), this song is diametrically opposed to 'La Belle P.', which is in a major key and speaks of life, joyful egotism and having many lovers.[27] It is entirely fitting then that Cléo's 'personal soundtrack' in the second half of the film should be a theme on 'Un Cri d'Amour', and this starts as soon as she leaves her apartment, but had been anticipated by the extraordinary scene in *Chapter 7* when her diegetic performance of 'Un Cri d'Amour' gradually segues into an anti-realistic (and hyper-real) orchestral and reverberating rendition of the song's last few stanzas, all recorded in one take. How are we to interpret this? We know that this song (or at least its lyrics) is new to Cléo, yet at one point, she ceases to read the lyrics, as if improvising with her own lyrics. The morbid lyrics become conflated with her latent thoughts at that time and Varda succeeds in accurately conveying how lyrics can profoundly affect people, either performers or listeners, through their uncanny parallels.

It would appear that all the non-diegetic music in the film is the soundtrack playing in Cléo's mind. As Antoine jokingly mentions on the bus in *Chapter 13*, she is indeed a 'mélomane', not (just) in the sense of a person who appreciates music, but someone who loves melodrama. When José visits her in *Chapter 5*, we hear a new melody which is not related to either 'La Belle P.' or 'Un Cri d'Amour'. It is simply called 'The Lovers' Theme' and inspired by Paul Delmet's style. Delmet was a singer and songwriter who was very popular at the end of the nineteenth century for his old-fashioned and sickly love songs.[28] Betsy Ann Bogart, in her thesis on the music in Varda's films, argues that '[i]n a formal, classical style, in the key of E major, and in regular 4/4 time, it expresses the narrative point of view of Cléo's lover, who views her in the stereotyped role of mistress'.[29] This is an attractive theory, but I doubt very much that the merely 'decorative' José is granted any point of view whatsoever in the film. Even if he were, his personal soundtrack would probably be work-related… It is far more likely to be the soundtrack of how Cléo aspires to see herself and her relationship, namely in an idealistic and excessively romantic way. The soft-focus, 'pastel' images and saccharine music jar with the obvious lack of intimacy between the pair (highlighted by their restlessness and conflicting positions on the bed, where eye contact is egregiously absent), causing much tension and resulting in possibly the most uncomfortable sequence in the entire film.

All the other music in the film is diegetic: Cléo's song, 'La Belle P.' in the taxi and on the jukebox; the honky-tonk music heard when Dorothée and Cléo leave the cinema after the short film and which had been written by Michel Legrand for several of the Eldorado cabaret scenes in *Lola*; the few bars of a mandolin redolent of Italy, heard, appropriately, when Antoine and Cléo's bus passes the Place d'Italie. Music in *Cléo de 5 à 7*, then, can reflect subjective states in the same way as visual POV or internal monologue. Let us now turn to characterisation in the film.

The Spoilt Child, the Maid-cum-Madam and the Chatterbox: characters in *Cléo de 5 à 7*

During the brief time that we spend in Cléo's company, we may on occasion feel supremely irritated by her character (and possibly others as well…). However, this should on no account undermine our enjoyment of the film, or its success. After all, we wouldn't dream of dismissing masterpieces of literature simply on the grounds that their protagonists are irritating or have some sort of tragic flaw.

We soon discover that we are not alone in negatively judging Cléo: most of the other characters are critical of her as well. She is accused of being childish or a spoilt child several times (by Angèle, Bob and Dorothée) and *capricieuse* – capricious or fickle – (by Angèle and Bob). Bob in particular is brutally honest but also bitterly snide and hints that she has no talent and her moderate success is based merely on her connections, and possibly her looks.

Film critics have called Cléo an airhead and a silly goose, yet at no point in the film does Cléo say or do anything downright stupid. Her conversation may at times be banal or superficial, but it is never inane or ignorant, only *self*-ignorant. In fact, there is very little that we can derive about her from her dialogue, even her interior monologue does not shed much light on her deeper self. Corinne Marchand's gestures, on the other hand, are fascinatingly eloquent.

Cléo moves elegantly and her gestures are mostly exquisitely graceful and devoid of brusque movements, yet in the first half of the film, she can be surprisingly and noticeably clumsy. This is not innocent on Marchand's part and expresses Cléo's egotism and lack of consideration. Given Varda's precision in her *mise-en-scène*, I do not believe that this gaucheness was in any way accidental.

In *Chapter 1*, when Cléo leaves the tarot reader's building, she opens the door onto the street and omits to close it behind her, leaving the building vulnerable to hawkers and tramps. The tone is set: Cléo (who is seldom alone) expects someone else to close it after her. Later, during Angèle's anecdote in the café in *Chapter 2*, having ordered a coffee, Cléo proceeds to stir it so clumsily that it slops all over the saucer and table. An attentive waiter rushes up to wipe the table, but Cléo does not apologise or even look contrite. Then at the hatter's, she is the classic 'shopper-from-hell', wanting to try everything on and demolishing the displays with no consideration for the shop assistants. In fact, whereas Cléo can be coquettishly flirtatious with male staff (the café waiter), she can be downright rude to female staff (the shop assistant; the taxi driver), leaving it to Angèle to bid them goodbye. Finally, Cléo behaves offhandedly towards another female, Angèle; in *Chapter 5*, she kicks off her shoes and divests herself onto the floor. It is clear that Angèle is used to picking up after Cléo, but the gesture is nevertheless eloquent in showing how Cléo treats Angèle, i.e. not as an equal (let alone a mother figure here), but as an inferior, a mere maid. There ends Cléo's 'clumsiness', which is by all accounts deliberate and therefore even more insulting to others. In the second half of the film, Cléo is a changed woman: her gestures are precise, accurate and considerate, like those of a grown woman and not a sloppy child. She no longer treats others like inferiors but like equals.

Corinne Marchand's performance is interesting in the context of the New Wave since New Wave actors' gestures were often encouraged to be clumsy to convey authenticity. In her chapter on Jeanne Moreau and New Wave actresses, Ginette Vincendeau notes that '[i]t was important that actors and actresses were not seen to act [...]'.[30] But gaucheness of course draws attention to itself and so becomes another kind of performance that results in an ironic slippage, a gap between performance and character: 'What seems to me most characteristic of New Wave acting,' argues Vincendeau, 'is the *combination* of authenticity and décalage [displacement, slippage, hiatus], which parallels the filmmakers' paradoxical drive to realism and personal expression.'[31] However, even though New Wave acting was by no means as improvised as it appeared, the acting had an added dimension in *Cléo* since Corinne Marchand's gestures (whether clumsy or not) were precisely orchestrated by Varda. Varda's direction of actors always concentrates on concrete gestures and behaviour. As Sandy Flitterman-Lewis argues, 'Rather than focusing on the psychologies of the characters, Varda prefers to describe an attitude, a gesture, a manner. It is this materialist conception of acting, linked perhaps to the influence of Bachelard, which permits her to attain an acting style concomitant with her overall social conception.'[32] Thus the realism

Cléo's disregard for Angèle: undressing onto the floor (22.39).

in Marchand's performance lies in the fact that Cléo's 'clumsiness' is so patently inauthentic, since we soon realise that Cléo *herself* is playing a part, that of the Spoilt Princess who can afford to spill her coffee, drop clothes onto the floor, but who can cease to be clumsy whenever she chooses, simply because gaucheness no longer becomes her new persona. This inauthenticity has an Existentialist resonance, which will be explored in greater detail in the next section.

The nature of Cléo and Angèle's relationship is intriguing, not least because of a rather egregious gap in the story: we never discover how, when and where the two women met, and who Angèle is in relation to Cléo: is she a maid, a housekeeper, a confidante, a chaperone, a secretary, a personal assistant, or a mixture of all of the above? Varda describes her in the screenplay as a 'maid – godmother – confidante, a bit of a brothel madam, a bit of an auntie-figure ['un peu maquerelle, un peu tata']'.[33] Before we meet Angèle at the end of *Chapter 1*, she has already been verbally introduced through Irma's description of her as the Dame de Pique (Queen of Spades) in the Mademoiselle Lenormand tarot deck; Irma is curiously negative: she sees an older woman, a widow, 'who is perhaps not very scrupulous when it comes to running your life, but who's very devoted to you'.[34] Cléo acquiesces, 'yes, it's true', but whether she agrees with the former part of Irma's statement is another matter; she certainly doesn't refute it. Irma continues, 'She took you away from your family and your home town towards a more emancipated life which enabled you to meet a very generous man.' This rules out Angèle's possible chaperone aspect and makes her sound more like a *mère maquerelle*, a brothel madam. It is not entirely clear what Irma means by Angèle not being terribly scrupulous in running Cléo's life: is Angèle exploiting Cléo financially or is she exerting a morally negative influence over her, and if so, in what way? We will never learn Irma's personal definition of unscrupulousness.

When we first encounter Angèle in the café, she seems a benign character, though overly protective of Cléo. Subtly and gradually, however, it transpires that Angèle is an evil and manipulative presence; it is no accident that Cléo feels better and happier in her absence. I do not think it excessive to compare Cléo to heroines gradually being poisoned by their husbands in films such as *Suspicion* (Alfred Hitchcock, 1941) or *Notorious* (Hitchcock, 1946), or whose husbands convince them that they are going mad (*Gaslight*, George Cukor, 1944). Angèle is not poisoning Cléo literally, but figuratively; she is corrupting and controlling her young and malleable mind using two formidable weapons: superstition and a rigid moral code based on outdated and conservative rules of behaviour around men.

Angèle often chides Cléo, particularly in front of others, in quite a humiliating manner. In the café, when Cléo orders a coffee, Angèle responds with, 'You know very well that coffee will make you more agitated. No coffee.' Whereas Cléo consistently uses the 'tu' form when addressing Angèle, Angèle alternates between 'tu' and 'vous' to address her employer. Here she uses 'tu', despite being in a public place: 'Tu sais bien que ça va encore t'énerver, le café.' At the hatter's, she treats Cléo like a naughty child, criticising her inappropriate choice of hat ('Fur? In this season? Don't be silly, Cléo!' ['Cléo, voyons!']). But her admonishing peaks when Cléo decides to purchase the fur hat and insists on keeping it on, thus committing the cardinal sin of wearing a new item of clothing on a Tuesday (a superstition I have never heard of). Angèle goes so far as to remove the hat from Cléo's head in front of the shop assistant. In a hushed and menacing tone, she says (using 'tu', after having previously used 'vous'), 'Tu ne veux pas attirer le malheur, non?' ('You're asking for trouble'), to which Cléo merely pouts. In both scenes, Angèle takes on the role of an indispensable lifesaver, and hints that Cléo's choices are not just irresponsible, but downright fatal: if she dies of cancer, it'll be because she didn't heed some obscure superstition, not because of abnormal cell growth. If Angèle were a man, alarm bells would start ringing in the audience's mind; he would appear guilty of non-physical domestic violence in the form of mental cruelty.

This said, Angèle's conversation with the female taxi driver in *Chapter 4* reveals that she admires strong, independent women. 'You're smart and gutsy,' she tells her. When Cléo and Angèle cross the courtyard to Cléo's apartment,

Angèle remarks that the taxi driver is a *typesse* ('character'), but Cléo misinterprets this and answers, 'You said it, it was shocking.' Angèle corrects her, saying that she found her brave and charming, and not shocking. Cléo appears to have become conditioned (by Angèle?) into finding feisty women vulgar and contemptible.

Finally, the Cléo–Angèle stand-off comes to a head on moral grounds in *Chapters 6* and *7*. Angèle is attentive (helping Cléo get undressed, preparing a hot-water bottle), but her advice about men is rigid and old-fashioned: 'Don't say you're ill. Men hate illness.' After José has left, Angèle praises Cléo for keeping her illness quiet. When Cléo expresses her profound dissatisfaction with José (confirmed through her eye contact with Angèle in the two-shot, on her words 'Do you think he loves me?'), Angèle is dismissive of her fears and defends José simply on the grounds that he spoils and respects her, takes her out and is generous. Finally, she argues that he's tall enough for Cléo, hinting that Cléo's above-average height may somehow make her less of a catch. Angèle stresses mostly José's material and physical qualities, but Cléo is more concerned with the fact that she cannot open up to him, something that Dorothée will later remark upon ('Love is all you need to confide'). Angèle then agrees with Cléo that José is selfish, and that she's too good to men, but seems resigned to this as if it were just one of those things in life.

In *Chapter 7*, after singing 'Un Cri d'Amour', Cléo sees the light and realises, among other things, that she is being exploited by her entourage: 'You're exploiting me!' It dawns on her that she is being kept ignorant (Bob never taught her how to read music) so as to remain dependent. After she has changed into her black dress, an interesting choreography between Angèle and Cléo indicates a radical shift in their relationship. A medium long shot records Cléo, partly hidden by two pillars and vases in the centre of the frame, moving away from the dressing table towards the camera. Angèle enters screen left, towards Cléo, but passes between the two pillars. Cléo makes a sharp left, as if to avoid Angèle. 'Do you want me to come?' asks Angèle. Cléo briefly disappears behind a pillar and continues to move left as Angèle moves right. Cléo then seems to remember something and turns to face right and returns to the dressing table to quickly pick up the fur hat she has been forbidden to wear. 'No, I want to be alone,' she replies. Angèle stops as if to keep her distance, as if suddenly afraid of Cléo's unpredictability. As Cléo moves left again, Angèle follows, mirroring her movements, though still keeping her distance. This choreography clearly expresses Cléo's spatial emancipation from Angèle's clutches. Cléo's movements lead, Angèle timidly follows. Cléo's decision to wear the hat on a Tuesday ('Damn Tuesday, I'll do as I please!') is a strong act of defiance vis-à-vis Angèle's superstitious rules.

Superstition is rife in the film. The tarot reading in the credits sequence sets the tone: these women are dependent on the irrational, the unscientific, the unproven. Their lives are governed by spurious rules and objects: new clothes on Tuesdays, 'unlucky' cab number plates, hats on beds, broken mirrors (two of them), 13 chapters... There is even evidence of non-Western superstition in the form of two 'Hand of Fatima' amulets: one hanging on the wall of Cléo's apartment and the other on the window sill to the left of the displayed jewellery.[35] Spectators may have ambivalent responses to this unquestioning belief in the occult: on the one hand, Angèle's superstition is laughable, but on the other hand, we may be culturally conditioned to accept the broken mirror as ominous of Cléo's untimely demise. Last but not least, there is no denying how uncannily and unerringly *correct* Irma's reading is: everything she predicts happens. Unprompted, she flawlessly identifies Cléo as a musician, she spots her illness through the card representing the doctor. She mentions Bob (first card), Angèle (second), José (fourth and fifth) in detail. If she fudges her interpretation of the first deck, it is because it is almost impossible to interpret without prior knowledge of Cléo's circumstances. In the second deck, she identifies Antoine as 'a talkative young man who'll amuse you'. However, she glibly refuses to engage in morbid predictions; in the first deck, the card traditionally known as representing death, the Ace of Spades, appears, yet she does not mention it. In the second deck, the impact of the Marseilles tarot equivalent, the 'Arcane Sans Nom' (known as Death in English), is so obvious (a partly skeletal body) that she

Cléo and Angèle's stand-off (39.42).

cannot gloss over it, yet she nevertheless minimises its significance by arguing that it really means 'a complete transformation of your entire being'. This is accurate, except that combined with the preceding card, the Tower, it is a very ominous card indeed, signifying 'imminent catastrophe'.[36] Individually, all the cards in the second deck represent change, renewal, a symbolic spring, but combined, they spell death. Although Irma doesn't go into much detail about the meaning of the Hanged Man, this is a crucial card: it represents widened consciousness, and seeing the world from a different and alienating angle (namely upside down, which may be uncomfortable), which is the subject of the film in a nutshell. Significantly, Varda's choice of opening with a somewhat disorientating overhead shot of cards and disembodied hands reinforces this feeling of alienation and forces the spectator to see things from a new and unexpected angle. It is as close as Varda could get to an upside-down shot, which would perhaps have been too quirkily experimental for the narrative.

Varda does not seem to have much time for such pursuits, hence her decision to shoot this sequence, or at least the overhead shots of the cards, in colour. Varda sees the cards as an 'illustration' of life and not to be confused with black and white 'reality'.[37] Yet, there is no doubt by the end of the film that if Irma's reading has been accurate thus far, then, chillingly, her reading of Cléo's palm disclosed only to her husband ('I saw cancer. She is doomed') must be correct too. I do not believe, however, that Varda is out to prove that superstitions are nonsense, but that living one's life rigidly by them is a denial of free agency and of life experienced to the full. It is a form of

Seeing the world upside down and through a broken mirror (60.19).

self-imprisonment and oppression, a yoke. This is nothing new in film: superstiousness often highlights a female character's covert entrapment. Archetypal *femme fatale* Gilda (Rita Hayworth) seems free of moral constraints and guilt, but is tormented by superstition (*Gilda*, Charles Vidor, 1946). In Truffaut's *Jules et Jim* (1962), Catherine (Jeanne Moreau) also displays superstitious behaviour (hats on beds), despite her apparently free and wild existence. There is something specifically and culturally 'feminine' about this superstitious behaviour. Superstition is derided by society because of its lack of scientific basis, yet it is also used as a way of controlling women, often by women themselves.

Through Angèle's character, *Cléo de 5 à 7* is not so much critical of patriarchy as of a form of *matriarchy* that is far more insidious, controlling and destructive. A *woman* is Cléo's worst enemy. For whatever reason (envy, jealousy…), Angèle is bent on keeping Cléo as a living doll. She disapproves of Cléo's desire to empower herself and be rid of her inadequate lover. She dislikes it when she tries to think for herself and imposes rigid rules of conduct on her. The film's warning against matriarchy still has currency to this day and is a stroke of feminist (and visionary) genius on Varda's part. Current popular culture is still teeming with intelligent and successful women who are slaves to superstition – Charlotte (Kristin Davis) consulting various (female and venal) psychics to discover whether she'll ever get married in *Sex and the City*[38] – or who follow rigid rules of behaviour in self-help books – consulted by Bridget Jones, who finally decides to bin them all and free herself of bad

Looking at the world upside down: the Hanged Man (2.50).

advice at the end of Helen Fielding's novel *Bridget Jones: The Edge of Reason*, 2001. British women's magazines have whole pages devoted to ads for healers, tarot readers and psychics, all just a premium-rate call away. More alarmingly, in 1995, the dating handbook *The Rules* by Ellen Fein and Sherrie Schneider proved a runaway bestseller, with such edicts as 'Don't Accept a Saturday Night Date After Wednesday' (Rule 7) or 'Don't Open Up Too Fast' (Rule 19), in other words 'Play Hard to Get' and 'Don't Be Yourself', which could have been written by Angèle herself.[39]

Moving on to Antoine-the-Chatterbox, although he is the antithesis of Cléo in many ways (he is spontaneous, outgoing, fearless, talkative, ordinary, male), he may elicit a similar response to her in the viewer: he is irritating at first until we discover more about him, and he changes noticeably. At first, Antoine appears to be the classic *dragueur*, a man who chats up lone women indiscriminately. When he approaches Cléo at the waterfall, he invades her personal space; she soon edges away, only for him to follow and reinvade her space, leaning over to force her to face him. The flatness of her responses to his banal gambits, 'Do you like the sound of water?' and 'It's quiet here, isn't it?', indicates that she is used to such lines and not impressed by them. But is Cléo making the same assumption about his intentions as we are? His words have nothing flirtatious about them; it is only his manner that is clumsily intrusive. He succeeds in gradually encouraging her to turn away from her preoccupations and the waterfall and notice the park and its unusual absence of children. Antoine, by his own admission, is inquisitive and incites others to be inquisitive too. He is thus the perfect match for Cléo at that precise

The mirrored foyer performance (5.20).

moment. In that respect, it is fate that brings them together, although Varda did not want their encounter to be interpreted as romantic in any way: 'It's not at all a meeting of two exceptional beings, or fate, or the "we were destined to meet" aspect.'[40] Varda critiqued reviews which assumed that Cléo and Antoine's incipient relationship was one of burgeoning love: 'In films, the only thing we are able to accept in a woman is her relationship with love – is she or is she not in love; has she been in love, or will she be in love. Even if she is alone, she *has* been in love or she should be or she would like to be in love.'[41] Towards the end of *Chapter 13*, Cléo and Antoine may appear happy and comfortable together (Cléo seems rid of her anxiety and Antoine is able to keep silent), but they never kiss, and tellingly, Antoine introduces himself to the doctor as her brother. Irma was correct in identifying him as 'Le Bateleur' (The Magician) and not 'L'Amoureux' (The Lovers, plural, in English): The Magician represents spring, renewal and vitality, he is often a brother and/or a somewhat clumsy and callow adolescent.[42] He is categorically not a lover. And it is precisely a surrogate family that Cléo urgently needs, not yet another boyfriend.

All in all, the characters in *Cléo de 5 à 7* are more complex than they at first appear. Angèle in particular is not as benign as she seems. It is not just Cléo who changes in the course of the film but Angèle and Antoine also mutate through their interaction with the changing Cléo. I now propose to show how the film illustrates certain tenets of Existentialism, particularly through the notion of (self-)awareness.

Antoine invades Cléo's personal space (67.26).

Cléo de 5 à 7 as a filmic illustration of the Existentialist zeitgeist

The New Wave emerged at a time when Existentialism, by which I mean Jean-Paul Sartre's version, was the dominant philosophy in France. Many New Wave films inevitably took Existentialist concepts on board, though in mainly lay and accessible terms. Some films became exponents of Sartrean Existentialism, and *Cléo de 5 à 7* is undoubtedly one of them.

Precursors to Existentialism had been around since the nineteenth century and early twentieth century, with Søren Kierkegaard, Friedrich Nietzsche and Martin Heidegger. Nietzsche had famously declared in *The Gay Science/Die fröhliche Wissenschaft* (1882) that 'God is dead'. This would lead to the main Existentialist tenet that, if there is no God, then human beings have no reason or justification for existing, and they are also totally free. The world is fundamentally meaningless and 'absurd', and total freedom can be a terrible, anxiety-ridden burden. This feeling of the futility of life intensified after the Second World War, and there was an overall sense in Western culture that traditional moral and social values had disintegrated, hence the appeal of Existentialism in the 1940s and 1950s. There was no longer a hope of bringing about a better world through human effort and endeavour. This disenchantment was felt in literature (mainly Sartre and Albert Camus), but also in film. Hollywood was no longer making films like *It's a Wonderful Life* (Frank Capra, 1946), which showed that the common good could yield results, a very Utilitarianist view.[43] Rather, it was more interested in the Existentialist rebel in films such as *The Wild One* (László Benedek, 1954) and *Rebel Without a Cause* (Nicholas Ray, 1955), starring Marlon Brando and James Dean respectively, characters who were free in the sense that their actions were not determined by traditional or social values.

It has often been argued that Michel Poiccard (Jean-Paul Belmondo) in Godard's *À bout de souffle* (1960) is the ultimate Existentialist hero of the New Wave. He is a rebel, he appears to be totally free, the master of his own fate, but in fact, he is constantly playing a role: that of 'rebel', 'gangster' and 'lover'. Similarly, Patricia (Jean Seberg) takes on the role of the 'American in Paris', the *femme fatale* and the 'informer'. She thinks she is free, but she is conditioned by her social background. Her 'Bonnie and Clyde' fantasy is not sustainable in a world where parents subsidise one's Parisian journalism course and an unwanted pregnancy is a very real risk. As many have pointed out, Michel is considerably influenced by popular culture.[44] He adopts Humphrey Bogart's mannerisms and plays a variety of roles, even to his death. His identity is unstable and shifting, just like his many passport alter egos.[45]

In *L'Être et le néant/Being and Nothingness* (1943), Sartre examined in depth the problem of our inescapable self-awareness. Sartre argued that the proof of human freedom is that we are able to detach ourselves from our immediate physical environment and use our powers of imagination. We do not merely *exist*, like plants or rocks. We also have the ability to experience *essence*, i.e. what we become. We are free to make choices that can change the course of our lives. In other words, as Sartre put it, existence precedes essence. We *exist* before we make choices to *be*. However, this freedom also means that we are constantly aware of and questioning ourselves; we are literally 'self-conscious'. Because of this permanent state of consciousness, or what Sartre terms the *pour-soi*, or 'for-itself', we cannot entirely *be* what we are, we cannot attain the *en-soi*, or 'in-itself'. Ideally, we would be totally ourselves (*en-soi*) while remaining *aware* that we are being ourselves (*pour-soi*). But one state cancels out the other. A possible solution is to *play* at being ourselves, but this behaviour is of course inauthentic. One of the best-known passages in *L'Être et le néant* concerns a café waiter who is so uncertain of his own identity that he plays at being a café waiter. He is never spontaneous and genuine. The same could be said of Cléo, particularly in the first half of the film.

Sartre describes this waiter's behaviour and gestures as patently exaggerated: 'His movement is quick and forward, *a little too* precise, *a little too* rapid. He comes towards the patrons with a step *a little too* quick'[46] (my italics). '[...] he is playing at *being* a waiter in a café. [...] The game

Wrenching off the wig/mask (39.35).

is a kind of marking out and investigation. [...] The café waiter plays with his condition in order to *realize* it.'[47] However, Sartre points out that this play-acting goes beyond mere social positions: 'I am never any one of my attitudes, any one of my actions. [...] The attentive pupil who wishes to *be* attentive, his eyes riveted on the teacher, his ears open wide, so exhausts himself at playing the attentive role that he ends up by no longer hearing anything.'[48]

From the outset of *Cléo de 5 à 7*, it is clear that Cléo is constantly play-acting. How can we tell? Indeed, if we have no prior knowledge of Corinne Marchand's histrionic talents, we can be forgiven for thinking she is merely a poor actress: her sobbing at the fortune-teller's sounds fake, yet her tears are real. In the café in *Chapter 2*, again, she cries in an exaggerated manner, and while looking into a mirror to boot, as if trying to duplicate the effect on her café audience (Angèle, the café owner and a waiter). At the hatter's, when her name is recognised, she simpers in false modesty. Likewise in the taxi when her song is playing on the radio, Cléo orders the taxi driver to switch it off supposedly because the recording is 'awful'. Generally speaking, in the first half of the film, Cléo is always play-acting when others are present (discounting Angèle, who is after all her confidante): she is shown to be extremely conscious of the gaze of others. But occasionally, she goes to the extreme of play-acting when she is alone (for example in the entrance hall to the fortune-teller's building, when she admires her repeated reflections in

Parc Montsouris: Cléo's solo performance (65.36).

the mirror, or a playful moment when she descends some steps in the Parc Montsouris as if she were in a revue).

We know that this is not the result of poor acting skills for two reasons: Cléo's behaviour changes radically in *Chapter 7*, as soon as she wrenches off the 'mask' of her wig, and continues until the end of the film. Secondly, Varda mentions Cléo's (and not Marchand's) play-acting several times in the screenplay. In the 'Ça va, ça vient' café scene, Varda writes that 'Cléo cries and *plays* the martyr' (p. 24) (my italics). Later, at the hatter's, she 'puts on simpering airs and *plays* to the gallery [...]' (p. 28). And as mentioned earlier, Marchand's gestures, which are so patently clumsy in Part 1, are clearly intended to express Cléo's 'spoilt brat/diva' persona. Even Angèle is playing a part: 'One mustn't forget that Angèle loves Cléo with a sort of tender tyranny, she lends herself to the game.'[49]

There are other sequences where Existentialism is hinted at, but Varda seems to be turning it on its head: the taxi ride (*Chapters 3* and *4*) and the conversation between Cléo and Angèle in Cléo's apartment (*Chapter 5*). The notion of fate is strong throughout *Cléo*, from the tarot reading to the open-ended closing chapter. What stands out, however, in these two sequences is the subtle struggle between fate (embodied by the character of Angèle) and free will and choice (in the budding 'transformed' Cléo). After the hatter's, Cléo and Angèle go to find a cab on the rue de Rivoli. During the ride, the camera alternates from two-shots to frontal shots of the road from behind the driver's right shoulder interspersed with a few shots of Cléo profile right. We cross the Pont Neuf to the Left Bank. Just after she has laughed in false modesty at her song being played on the radio, Cléo is shown in profile left and her eyes are drawn to something off-screen right. This is followed by a swish pan right to reveal what has caught her eye: a shop window of tribal African masks. Close-up of what appears to be two rather creepy (at least to non-Africans) death masks. This is very plausible and realistic since we are now on the rue Guénégaud, a street teeming with art galleries and shops, with quite a few specialising in 'primitive' art. Given Cléo's state of mind, it makes sense that she picks up references to death. Angèle and the taxi driver are chatting off-screen about Cléo's song and do not seem to have noticed the masks. Cut to a medium close-up of Cléo in profile right; she slowly turns her head back to face ahead and looks glum, pensive and, yes, slightly queasy. Off-screen, Angèle asks her if she's all right, to which Cléo answers that she feels 'nauseous' ('j'ai mal au cœur') and leans out of the window. Significantly, the taxi driver asks her if the music is not helping, to which Cléo answers: 'No.' Clearly, this feeling of nausea has been brought on by the masks, by the reminder of death, by a world that is very much alien to her safe and cosy pop singer's life, but it is not being alleviated by (her own) music.

Sartrean Existentialism is totally atheist. As Sartre suggested in his 1938 novel *La Nausée/Nausea*, if God is absent, then there is no reason for anything to exist at all. This futility and gratuity of life makes the protagonist of *La Nausée*, Antoine Roquentin, feel perpetually nauseous. The fundamental absurdity of existence disgusts him and everything appears viscous, fluid and unstable. Roquentin spends a good deal of time in a café which has a jukebox with a record of Sophie Tucker singing 'Some of these Days'. This music gives him temporary respite from his nausea and drives him to conclude that art releases him from the absurdity and nauseating excess of existence. Art lives on beyond existence, it is not just a mere physical artefact. Roquentin finally finds salvation through art, more specifically through writing.

However, the art of the masks and of the pop song does not alleviate Cléo's anguish; it in fact contributes to her nausea. It may remind her of the finitude of her own existence, something that she had probably never had to consider before. Yet, it can also be seen as positive, since it jolts her into a new perceptual dimension: would Cléo have noticed these morbid artefacts before? Cléo is an artist of sorts since she is a singer (even though she does not write her own songs). Moreover, she moves in artistic circles: she lives on the predominantly artistic Left Bank and her friends (Dorothée, Bob, Raoul) contribute to art in one way or another (sculpture/painting, music and cinema respectively). Yet art, particularly her own art, does not appear to save her from her own nausea and anxiety. When she visits the Dôme café in *Chapter 8*, the first thing she does is home in on the jukebox and put on her own song, 'La Belle P'. This rather brash and cheerful tune seems incongruous in the café at that precise moment. The Dôme patrons are shown sitting in groups and talking. In fact, Cléo is the only one who is not part of a group and is silent. She has begun to actively observe and listen to others. We in fact (as we can be certain she does too) overhear a female patron angrily telling her companion that the music is too loud. Clearly, no one seems remotely interested in her song, nor do they seem to pay any attention to her restless presence. As Varda writes, 'Cléo realises that her pop-singer's success is flimsy.'[50] Whereas Antoine Roquentin was aware of the perennity of art, of its existence beyond the confines of the contingent and material world, Cléo is acutely aware of the transience of a trite pop song. In *Chapter 7*, she even asks, 'What is a song? How long does it last?'

Varda does not mention *La Nausée* as a possible reference for *Cléo*, yet the actual mention of nausea ('j'ai mal au cœur' during the taxi ride) and the presence of the jukebox in the Dôme sequence seem more than merely coincidental. However, at the same time, *La Nausée* harks back to Rainer Maria Rilke's pre-Existentialist novel *The Notebook of Malte Laurids Brigge*, which Varda claims inspired her.

Also set on the Left Bank in Paris, though in the first decade of the twentieth century, *The Notebook of Malte Laurids Brigge* is a young Danish poet's first-person narration of both his immediate experience of living in a poverty-stricken area of Paris and his memories of his (more privileged) youth in Denmark. In Paris, all Brigge can see is death and illness. But when he recalls his Danish youth, it is also to speak of death and illness, particularly the prolonged death of his grandfather. Brigge alternates between hard, detached objectivity and introspective subjectivity. Faced with the terrible external reality of poverty, disease and death, Brigge finds himself powerless and non-existent. Worse still, it destroys his ability to create poetry. Brigge strives towards objective description by trying to emulate Charles Baudelaire, but can't help returning to a destructive subjectivity. His hope is that 'this totally alien outer world will become transformed into his inner world and then undergo a further transformation into something objective – a poem'.[51]

Cléo de 5 à 7 constantly oscillates between objectivity and subjectivity. Varda's intention had been to make a 'subjective documentary'. On the one hand, we have, in typical New Wave/*cinéma vérité* fashion, shots of real places, real people, real sounds, but we are also privy to Cléo's thoughts, anxieties, flashbacks, in short, her interiority through certain filmic strategies such as POV shots.

Aspects of the *mise-en-scène* cleverly highlight Cléo's shaky identity and self-awareness. Mirrors abound in the film, and not just as bad omens. In Part 1, Cléo's reflection is largely comforting to her (in the fortune-teller's foyer, at the hatter's, in her apartment) yet tellingly, some are not whole but either multiple (x 4 in the foyer) or split in two (by the seam in the 'Ça va, ça vient' café mirror). In Part 2, the Chinese restaurant mirror sends back a reflection that is no longer reassuring but opaque ('I can't see my own fears' as expressed in her interior monologue). Yet that very mirror, as we shall see in the next section, will offer a stepping stone to observing the world. Finally, and this is a very Existentialist idea, Cléo no longer needs a physical mirror for reassurance by the end of the film: the final shot shows her looking at Antoine as if into a mirror. This is strongly reminiscent of Sartre's play *Huis clos* (1944), in which three characters find themselves in Hell, which turns out to be a drawing room. There are no mirrors and this makes vain Estelle uneasy: 'When I don't see myself, even though I can feel myself, I'm not sure that I really exist.' Inès offers to be her mirror, but Estelle resents having to trust Inès's judgement.[52] Ultimately, we are nothing without the gaze of others, but that gaze is always subjective, and this is something Cléo has to learn and accept.

Finally, Existentialism stresses that we must embrace our freedom and not attempt to evade it through 'bad faith' (*mauvaise foi*). We must be responsible for our choices and actions, and not blame others or external circumstances. An example of 'bad faith' would be a workaholic who believes that s/he does not have the choice to work less because otherwise s/he would be letting others down or jeopardising the success of his/her company/ employer. It soon becomes clear that Cléo is by no means the mistress of her fate, or her choices, nor even of her love life. She lets Angèle rule her life, and in the first half of the film, Cléo is passive rather than active. However, we notice a change even before *Chapter 7*. In the sequence in her apartment, the conversation between Cléo and Angèle is very revealing: Cléo tentatively asserts her choices and opinions and begins to reject Angèle's 'brainwashing'. Cléo's 'bad faith' was to unquestioningly accept Angèle's advice and remain a pliable mistress. She is becoming uncompromising in her search for real love and aware that she needs to take responsibility for her actions. In order to do this, she needs to be alone and think for herself.

Antoine as mirror (85.45).

The loneliness of the *flâneuse*

Cléo de 5 à 7 is memorable for its urban walking, particularly solitary *female* urban walking, which is unusual in itself. In this section, I intend to define the nineteenth-century concept of *flânerie* and to determine whether Cléo is a *flâneuse*, and if so, whether she succeeds in subverting the male preserve of *flânerie*, or whether she in fact takes the idea of *flânerie* even further.

Flâner, flânerie, flâneur, flâneuse: none of these terms can be adequately translated into English. The nearest translation of *flâner* is 'to stroll' or 'to go for a stroll'. According to the French Robert dictionary, *flâner* means to 'walk without haste, randomly, while losing oneself to the sensation and spectacle of the moment'.[53] The English definition tends to focus more on the inactive quality of *flânerie*: 'Aimless strolling or lounging; idleness.'[54] The term *flâneur* has crept into the English language to describe a person, generally a man, who walks aimlessly in an urban setting (there is no such thing as a country *flâneur*) to revel in the urban spectacle and observe his fellow man (or woman). *Flânerie* must not have a purpose, nor must it be used to show off. The nineteenth-century dandy strolled *to be seen*. The true nineteenth-century *flâneur*, on the other hand, blended in with the crowd (Charles Baudelaire's version) or remained distanced from people and capitalist commodities (Walter Benjamin's take). In the Parisian and nineteenth-century sense, *flânerie* was by no means idle; on the contrary, it was an active pastime. In short, the key words one could use to sum up *flânerie* would be: mobility (but without haste and without a specific goal – one could not conceivably be a *flâneur* in a hurry to catch a train, for example); active observation (of people, window displays, architecture, etc.), something that is generally pleasurable; and modernity.

Cléo undertakes two main walks. Both are quite short but significant. The first one begins when Cléo has just left the fortune-teller's building on the rue de Rivoli. Buoyed by her confidence-boosting interaction with the foyer mirror, she liltingly saunters along the busy pavement. The camera records her in medium shot, becoming gradually closer, and from a slightly high angle, tracking right to reframe her. The pavements are partly taken over by the overspill from clothes shops: clothes rails, stalls, bins, etc. Mostly male 'rag traders' loiter outside their shops and stare appreciatively at Cléo's tall, striking and glamorous figure. There is the odd banter ('alors, on s'promène?' – 'so, taking a walk?') and flirty salesman's patter to which she responds as she is expected to: with coquettish reserve. She slows down only once, to let a bicycle pass while crossing a side street, but otherwise, her pace remains regular and purposeful. Of course, in the following sequence, it transpires that she was on her way to meet Angèle in a nearby café.

If we focus on her face, and her eyes in particular, we sense that she is observing very little. She does not stop to examine the wares, her eyes glide over people and produce as if they were invisible or just totally uninteresting to her. Is she still mulling over the tarot session? Her face is a mask and reveals nothing of her thoughts; it certainly does not display anxiety. These two shots are very Ophülsian,[55] by which I mean that they are at once very graceful (aided by the non-diegetic legato string ensemble arrangement of 'La Belle P.') and cluttered. Cléo's background is teeming with shop paraphernalia and goods, but her foreground is equally filled with stalls and awnings, which, despite the camera's elevated angle, occasionally block our view of Cléo. Nevertheless, Cléo is very much the centre of this sequence; she attracts our gaze, first by her poise (she knows how to shimmy in high heels) and her striking attire where whiteness/blondeness dominate a largely darker background.

Cléo is not a *flâneuse* here: first of all, she has a purpose – to meet Angèle and tell her about the fortune-teller; her strolling is not aimless or meandering. Secondly, she is not an active observer, on the contrary she is very much a passive object of the gaze – the combined gaze of the spectator and the diegetic onlookers. The sequence is composed of just two tracking shots with no POV shots to allow us access into Cléo's subjectivity. The clutter in front of the frame further heightens our feeling that we are observing Cléo voyeuristically, even though she is in a public place and clearly aware of being observed. The attention she receives does not seem to intimidate or annoy her, if anything it seems to bolster the narcissism of the previous scene in front of the mirror. In

Cléo's first walk (6.04).

short, she behaves far more like a female dandy (even though there is no such thing) than like a *flâneuse*. Finally, what of modernity? In its more usual sense, there is modernity in this scene through the realist contemporary portrayal of Paris. In typical New Wave fashion, Varda chose to 'go down into the street', as Marcel Carné advocated some 30 years earlier,[56] and filmed real people, real traffic and real shops. Cléo stands out here as a fake doll amidst the ethnographic realism – and modernity – of Paris. Indeed, New Wave film-makers tried to capture Paris at its most buzzing and modern, as the hub of Europe. Truffaut had filmed the streets of the area of his youth – Pigalle, Clichy and Montmartre – in *Les Quatre cents coups*. Godard captured the bustle and noise of Paris (which sometimes blocked out the dialogue) in the summer of 1959 in *À bout de souffle*. The New Wave was predominantly urban and Parisian, with most films featuring scenes that positively revelled in the beauty and energy of Paris, and the joys of strolling, or better still, driving, in Paris. The boys playing in the streets of Paris in *Les Quatre cents coups* (1959), and a lot of driving around Paris in Claude Chabrol's *Les Cousins* (1959), for instance. But urban walking in New Wave films (as indeed in most films, and most novels) is often symptomatic of despair: Pierre (Jess Hahn) in Rohmer's *Le Signe du lion* (1959) who is homeless for much of the film, for example.

Similarly, the concept of *flânerie* was firmly anchored in Paris. We tend to associate *flânerie* with Baudelaire and Benjamin, but as Anke Gleber has noted in her book *The Art of Taking a Walk*, *flânerie* pre-dated these two key writers by several decades: 'For most German writers of the early nineteenth century, the pursuit of such novel experiences inevitably involves a journey to cities, and not just any city but to Paris, the most advanced and pronouncedly modern city in Europe.'[57] In the mid-nineteenth century, Victor Fournel published a volume that detailed the joys of walking specifically in Paris, entitled *Ce qu'on voit dans les rues de Paris*.[58] Finally, Walter Benjamin, in a 1935 programme for his never completed *Arcades Project*, proclaimed Paris to be the capital of the nineteenth century.[59] So in terms of its representation of Paris, *Cléo de 5 à 7* squarely follows this tradition of Paris as the locus of modernity.

Thus, aside from the modernity criterion, Cléo is not a *flâneuse* in this sequence. But before we move on to the second walking sequence in the film, we must ask ourselves this question: does the *flâneuse*, i.e. the female of *flâneur*, actually exist? Grammatically, yes, but the concept doesn't. For Baudelaire, the *flâneur* was unequivocally male. Furthermore, a woman who wandered in public in the nineteenth century was automatically morally suspect. As Susan Buck-Morss has articulated, if women roamed the streets, they became 'streetwalkers', prostitutes, carnal commodities.[60] Or as Anne

The Rue Delambre walk: Cléo seen and Cléo seeing (46.11–46.22, 46.24).

Friedberg explains, 'Women were objects for consumption, objects for the gaze of the flâneur, or the poet who, like Baudelaire, would notice women as mere passersby.'[61] Certainly, in the nineteenth century, respectable middle-class women, or *femmes honnêtes*, could not freely roam the streets of Paris or they could be mistaken for *femmes publiques* (women who appeared in public, on the streets, and by extension, were available as commodities). The female writer George Sand was a keen *flâneuse*, but she had to disguise herself as a man.[62] However, as Friedberg has aptly detailed, new spaces began to emerge in the mid-nineteenth century, public spaces such as the department store (to whose rise Émile Zola devoted a novel, which bore the telling title of *Au bonheur des dames/The Ladies' Delight*, in 1883), or the amusement park, spaces where women could venture alone, unchaperoned and exist outside of the eternal mother/whore dichotomy. In other words, women needed a *purpose* to their *flânerie*, which contradicts the very idea of *flânerie*, which is supposed to be *aimless*. This said, women could use this socially acceptable purpose of shopping or walking in the park as a spurious excuse for getting out of the house. Female mobility was thus far less morally reprehensible or dangerous. Consequently, according to Friedberg, the *flâneuse* does exist, largely thanks to late nineteenth-century consumerism and capitalism. However, this mode of *flânerie* remained exclusively *diurnal*, as opposed to the far more masculine and risqué nocturnal variety.

Cléo's second walk is quite different to the first; for a start, she does not have a clear purpose, though she does admittedly decide to visit Dorothée after overhearing a couple of artists at the Dôme mention her modelling talents. We know that Cléo does not have to visit the Salpêtrière hospital for her medical results, since she previously told Angèle that the doctor had asked her to phone him that evening. So apart from looking in on Dorothée, something that was not planned anyway, Cléo has no purpose whatsoever. Secondly, here it is made clear that Cléo is actively observing. Varda gives us plenty of access to her visual and aural point of view. She is aware of herself (the sound of her footsteps seems exaggerated) and of others.

This is quite different to Lidia's (Jeanne Moreau) long aimless walk in Milan and its suburbs in Michelangelo Antonioni's *La Notte/The Night* (1961). Even though we see Lidia observing others, sometimes almost getting involved (watching a fight and intervening, or watching boys setting off rockets in the wasteland), we never hear her thoughts or see the city through her eyes. There isn't a single POV shot during her *flânerie*. This is taken further in Antonioni's next film, *L'Eclisse/The Eclipse* (1962), again interestingly involving a large amount of female *flânerie*, where Vittoria (Monica Vitti) is clearly aware of her (modern and ancient) Roman environment, but we are never privy to her point of view, in fact we feel even more detached from her than we did from Lidia.

The late 1950s and early 1960s seemed to be a time in film when female characters were an excellent means of conveying a general post-war societal malaise. This is often shown in aimless and random urban walks. These women are not just walking off some sort of personal crisis, but they are also quite literally 'adrift' in modern society, detached from their environment. Florence Carala (Jeanne Moreau) goes for a long, aimless and nocturnal walk in Paris when her lover Julien (Maurice Ronet) fails to show up in Louis Malle's *Ascenseur pour l'échafaud/Lift to the Scaffold* (1958). The very bourgeoise Madame Carala seems completely out of place wandering the streets at night. In Godard's *Vivre sa vie* (1962), the prostitute Nana (Anna Karina) drifts around (daytime) Paris like a lost soul, even though the streets should rightly feel hers. In Resnais's *Hiroshima mon amour* (1959), the film actress Elle (Emmanuelle Riva) wanders the streets of Hiroshima at night and is predictably mistaken for a prostitute. As previously mentioned, Antonioni likes his elegant heroines to do a lot of meandering in deserted urban landscapes, either hyper-modern fascist-era suburbs or wasteland, where they seem completely at odds. Conversely, male heroes in films of the 1950s and 1960s tend to favour fast and dangerous cars or motorbikes (Johnny (Marlon Brando) in László Benedek's *The Wild One*, 1954; Jim (James Dean) in Ray's *Rebel Without a Cause*, 1955; Michel Poiccard in *À bout de souffle*; Piero (Alain Delon) in *L'Eclisse*; and so on). Again, this is symptomatic of post-war tension (the fast car as plaything-cum-death wish rather than a means of getting from A to B), but in a very different, more violent way than the gentler female *flânerie*. Cléo's walk, seen in this rather despondent context, is more upbeat and therapeutic. Cléo is also adrift in a world that she neither knows well nor comprehends, but the walk seems to help her to see the world and herself more clearly, whereas Antonioni's female characters seem to sink further into an emotional void. In this sense, despite the film's urban location, Cléo is far closer to Jane Austen's heroines, whose brisk walks across fields would clear their heads (Elizabeth Bennet in *Pride and Prejudice* (1813), for example).

Cléo's 'walk' can be divided into several segments: from home to the Dôme; the Dôme (not a real walk, but let us not forget that *flânerie* could be conducted in cafés as well); from the Dôme to the sculptor's studio; the taxi ride and walk in the Parc Montsouris. Strictly speaking, part of the final segment is anomalous since Cléo is not physically alone: the taxi driver is present and does talk to her. However, he is a stranger to her and Varda's emphasis is still very much on Cléo's subjectivity. The segments with Dorothée cannot be included since Cléo is not alone, although of course, Dorothée does leave her briefly outside Montparnasse station to count sailors' pompoms…

The walk begins from the moment she emerges from her building into the courtyard. She passes a toddler idly tinkling on a toy piano. The rhythm of these couple of bars segues into the tempo of the non-diegetic music. It is the theme of 'Un Cri d'Amour', which caused her breakdown, but this time, it is played with just two instruments: a harp and plucked violin. The music signifies that Cléo is still caught up in the mood of the previous scene. Her facial expression reflects this: it is pensive and gloomy, and she does not yet appear to be aware of her surroundings. The camera tracks right as Cléo walks down the rue Huyghens to the junction with the boulevard Raspail. The rue Huyghens is deserted, except for three men standing in a doorway who watch her as she passes, but she does not seem to notice or acknowledge their presence. It is only when she reaches the junction that the music stops abruptly, cut short by pigeons fluttering away. It is at that moment that Cléo looks to her right and the camera swings round to reveal what caught her eye: a health food shop called 'Bonne Santé' ('Good Health'). This moment situates Cléo's nascent awareness and self-awareness. Next to the pharmacy, there is a Chinese restaurant with mirrors covered in Chinese ideogram in the window. Cléo approaches the one on the right, looks at her reflection, removes her hat, combs her hair and, in interior monologue, comments on what she sees: 'My unchanging doll's face… This ridiculous hat… I can't see my own fears. I thought everyone looked at me. I only look at myself. It wears me out.' But at that moment, she glimpses something behind her, in the mirror. We hear, and she obviously does too, a man loudly saying that we should not pity the frogs, for they do not suffer. Cléo looks round and the camera swings 180° to reach the source of the voice: it is a busker, surrounded by quite a large crowd of onlookers. Cléo is no longer wallowing in self-pity or gloomy thoughts; she has been distracted, pulled away from herself to observe the world. Naturally enough, intrigued, she walks over to the gathering. Reverse-angle of Cléo joining the crowd. Cut to what she sees: a man, in medium close-up, putting a live frog in his mouth, and swallowing it with some difficulty. Back to Cléo, looking on uncomfortably. The man walks past slowly, still ingesting his frog. This continues for several more frogs, until the busker finally vomits them all out, one by one, still alive, back into their tank. Varda inserts a couple of shots of 'real people' looking on, amused. The shots of Cléo, however, show her looking increasingly repulsed. Finally, when the busker vomits his first frog, she walks out of shot and a high-angle long shot shows her to be the only one to break away from the crowd and hastily turn the corner onto the Boulevard Montparnasse.

Repulsed she may be, but Cléo has taken her first step towards true *flânerie*: she has been distracted, sidetracked, she has behaved out of character (I doubt very much that Cléo is in the habit of watching buskers', acts), in other words, she has been taken out of herself, into the realm of observing others. Her first experience of observing others is not a pleasant one, and this repulsion continues after the Dôme with another busker, who is shown skewering his bicep. But it is her curiosity, her desire to look, that is crucial.

This is very reminiscent of another example of awakened female curiosity in the city, Virginia Woolf's modernist novel *Mrs Dalloway* (1925). Some reviewers have in fact remarked on both works' similar treatment of time. Jean-Louis Bory, for example, argues that *Cléo de 5 à 7* is as groundbreaking in its narrative technique as were Woolf's *Mrs Dalloway* or *To the Lighthouse* (1927), dubbing Varda 'the Virginia Woolf of modern cinema'.[63] However, in Woolf's novel, we are privy to the thoughts of Clarissa Dalloway throughout an entire day rather than just 90 minutes. Clarissa is not awaiting the result of a medical test, but on that day in June, a few years after the Great War, she is throwing a party for the political gentry. The egregious similarity between the two works is not so much the unity of time as the motif of female *flânerie*. In the opening chapter, Clarissa walks from Westminster to Bond Street. She does in fact have a goal in mind: to buy flowers for her party. But she could just as easily have left that task to a maid, or she could have taken a cab. Instead, she decides to walk, simply because she enjoys it. It is not clear whether she does this often or whether she even has the opportunity of doing this often. She admits this to an old acquaintance whom she meets in St James's Park; to his question 'Where are you off to?' she does not reveal a destination or purpose, but rather that 'I love walking in London. Really, it is better than walking in the country.'[64]

Her itinerary, like Cléo's, is very easy to follow and can be traced on a map. The walk would take about half an hour to an hour but is expanded by her thoughts, in stream of consciousness, some elated, some anxious. What is particularly relevant here is that her physical awareness of the topography of London is interwoven with her more abstract thoughts, resulting in a layering of exterior and interior lives:

> How much she wanted it – that people should look pleased as she came in, Clarissa thought *and turned and walked back towards Bond Street*, annoyed, because it was silly to have other reasons for doing things. Much rather would she have been one of those people like Richard [her husband] who did things for themselves, whereas, she thought, *waiting to cross*, half the time she did things not simply, not for themselves; but to make people think this or that; perfect idiocy she knew (*and now the policeman held up his hand*) for no one was ever for a second taken in. Oh if she could have had her life over again! she

thought, *stepping on to the pavement*, could have looked even differently!
(emphases mine).[65]

The Dôme sequence in *Cléo* is very similar, even though we do not hear Cléo's
thoughts. But we are made aware of her perception, her change in outlook,
her mental landscape, as well as the physical landscape of Paris, via POV shots
and aural point of view.

Paris: city of light and enlightenment

Paris is an essential component of *Cléo de 5 à 7*; indeed, the city is almost a
character in its own right. Varda preferred to linger on the Left Bank, and more
specifically the 14th arrondissement, by deciding that Cléo should live in the
rue Huyghens close to Vavin metro station. Traditionally, Paris has been
divided into two banks: the *rive droite* (Right Bank) and the *rive gauche* (Left
Bank). The former, or what could also be termed 'north Paris' (since the Île de
la Cité is the degree zero of all road distances in France, in the same way that
Charing Cross is in England), takes up two-thirds of Paris and is associated
with finance and business. It is the site of the Bourse, or Paris stock exchange,
the Banque de France, and the 'Sentier', or rag trade area in the 2nd and 10th
arrondissements. The Left Bank, on the other hand, constitutes just one-third
of Paris and comprises only six arrondissements out of 20. This bank is
considered more cultural and artistic. Not much has changed on the Left
Bank since the 1960s: it is still home to the École des Beaux Arts, several top
lycées such as Henri IV and Louis-le-Grand, prestigious Grandes Écoles
and universities (the École Normale Supérieure, the Collège de France, the
École Nationale d'Administration, Sciences-Po, the Sorbonne, the École de
Médecine...), major political institutions (the Assemblée Nationale and the
Sénat, the Hôtel Matignon, which is the Prime Minister's residence, and many
ministries). It is still teeming with publishing houses, bookshops and libraries,
with a recent and important addition being the huge state-of-the-art
Bibliothèque Nationale François Mitterrand in the 13th arrondissement.
Finally, as Antoine perceptively remarks (and Henry Miller before him), it is
also the bank with the most hospitals, the largest being the Pitié-Salpêtrière
in the 13th, where it may be remembered that Princess Diana was rushed
shortly before she died in August 1997, despite being involved in a car crash
on the Right Bank. It is entirely appropriate, then, that Cléo should reside on
the Left Bank, mingling with artists and within a stone's throw of a hospital.
It is also apposite that a character in a Varda film should live in the 14th
arrondissement, since this is where Varda herself has lived for the past 55 years.

Although Varda may have been daunted by Paris when she first arrived in the late 1940s, it is clear that she is cinematically fascinated by the French capital. Many of her films are set in Paris, but Varda is not interested in a touristy or artificial representation of Paris filled with clichéd landmarks. Rather, as Françoise Puaux has argued, Varda prefers to show the 'off-screen', the hidden side of Paris.[66] One of her very first shorts, *L'Opéra-Mouffe* (1958), showed the rue Mouffetard area in the 5th arrondissement (Left Bank again) as seen by a pregnant woman. In the 1950s, the rue Mouffetard was not the quaint market street that it is now (which is how Jean-Pierre Jeunet portrayed it in *Le Fabuleux destin d'Amélie Poulain*, 2001). It was an impoverished neighbourhood, and a bit of a *cour des miracles*, i.e. an area frequented by beggars and thieves. In the 'Quelques uns' segment, Varda is not afraid to show us real people: in close-up, we see tramps and drunks, ordinary people, old people wiping their faces and eyes or scratching. Just as in the 'De l'ivresse' section in *L'Opera-Mouffe*, we were shown tramps and drunks, asleep in the street or on benches. There is a Brassaï-like quality to these images, yet Varda is generally not interested in night-time Paris as Brassaï was.[67] In fact, Varda is more in the naturalistic tradition of Robert Doisneau and Henri Cartier-Bresson.[68] Varda tends to prefer natural daylight to artificial light in all her films, and this makes her a typical New Wave film-maker in terms of lighting practices.

Perhaps Varda's most affectionately urban film is *Daguerréotypes*, where she explores the lives of the shopkeepers on the street where she has lived for the past 50 years, the rue Daguerre near Denfert-Rochereau. It is an ethnographic study of half a dozen businesses owned by couples. Varda is the off-screen interviewer who asks them where they're from, how they met and what they dream about. None of them are originally from Paris but either emigrated from Algeria or Tunisia or came from the provinces, just like Varda herself. We do not see that much of the exterior reality of the street, but more of the (usually cramped and cluttered) shop interiors and shopkeepers. As usual, Varda is interested in a place via its inhabitants. 'By understanding people, one understands places better, and by understanding places, one understands people better,' she claims.[69] The film was also about herself at that time: 'It wasn't just about the people on my street, it was equally about what was going on in my head.'[70] Varda would later give some of these shopkeepers cameo roles in her fiction or non-fiction films, characteristically blending documentary realism and fictional worlds: the baker, Henri Piednoir, appears in *Jane B. par Agnès V.*, his wife Marie appears in *Une minute pour une image* and the Tunisian grocer appears in *Kung Fu master!*

As mentioned earlier, Varda's Paris is diurnal, not just in *Cléo*, as a direct result of its strict time-frame, but in all her films. Night-time scenes are rare. I doubt that this was for technical reasons, for that wouldn't explain why even her more recent and technically sophisticated films shun the night. It seems to be more of a thematic concern. Characters of the night are not ordinary enough, they are extraordinary, they do not lead the simple, banal, everyday – and yet fascinating – lives that Varda prefers to record: the fishermen in *La Pointe courte*, the carpenter, the seamstress and the postal worker in *Le Bonheur*, the shopkeepers in *Daguerréotypes*, the gleaners and marginal types of *Les Glaneurs et la glaneuse* are all at their most alive and interesting in the daytime. Even Mona (Sandrine Bonnaire) in *Sans toit ni loi*, who is perhaps the least 'ordinary' character in Varda's filmography given her choice of a solitary and nomadic lifestyle, sensibly chooses to walk during daylight hours and sleep at night. Even the sex scenes in *Le Bonheur*, whether marital or adulterous, are almost exclusively diurnal.

Cléo is no ordinary character and this is no ordinary hour and a half, yet the narrative is embedded in an ordinary and realist Paris, shot in the daytime, recording real people on the streets, sometimes staring quizzically straight into the camera, and this is one of the hallmarks of Varda's cinema. Yet, at the same time, it is typical of New Wave cinema which shot the city in a refreshingly realist way, though this was in fact not completely new, but a throwback to the early days of silent cinema (cf. the Lumière brothers, for

The clock at Irma's (4.06).

instance). However, Varda also likes to show nature, even in an urban film like *Cléo*, and nature is often portrayed as malevolent.

Nature and death

If, as Puaux has suggested, Varda does not romanticise the city, nor can she be accused of idealising the countryside. She is very much aware of the 'ferocity of nature', though portrays country people sympathetically (cf. *Les Glaneurs et la glaneuse*, for instance).[71] In many of her films (*Le Bonheur* being the exception), Varda chose to portray the darker and more sinister side of nature, which is often shown to be ugly, inhospitable, if not deadly. The Languedoc-Roussillon of *Sans toit ni loi* is cruel and cold and ultimately a partial cause of Mona's death; the beaches in *Les Créatures, Ulysse* – featuring a photograph of a naked man, a little boy and a dead goat (Saint-Aubin-sur-Mer on the Channel) – and *Sans toit ni loi* do not evoke the holidays: they are deserted, cold and unenticing. In *Ulysse*, the presence of the dead goat reminds us that death is omnipresent in nature. Dead animals are a recurring motif in Varda's films, not just the ones killed by humans for food (the catches of the day in *La Pointe courte* and *Les Créatures*; the carcasses and offal on display at the market in *L'Opéra-Mouffe*), but also those that presumably died from natural causes: several dead cats (*La Pointe courte*; *Les Créatures*), a dead bird and a dead goat in *Ulysse*. Finally, there is an inordinate amount of references to human death, though this may not appear striking because Varda

The clockmaker on the rue de Rivoli (14.54).

does not morbidly dwell on death but interweaves it as a normal and expected part of life. Death tends to occur on the sidelines (the death of a villager's child in *La Pointe courte*, for instance), and Varda avoids killing off her characters. Of course, the two notable exceptions to this are *Le Bonheur* and *Sans toit ni loi*, where the female protagonists die, with both deaths ambiguously straddling the fine line between accident and suicide.

If the possibility of Cléo's death is constantly mooted, Varda was not interested in showing us her possible demise. The fact that we will never know whether she recovers or not makes us more aware of Cléo's *life* and the remarkable shift that occurs during that crucial hour and a half. There are no dead animals at all in *Cléo de 5 à 7*, not even a butcher's or a fishmonger's stall, yet the film is brimming with references to death: aside from the obvious references during Madame Irma's reading, there is Angèle's anecdote in *Chapter 2* about a man whom doctors believed was doomed, the shop that Angèle and Cléo pass on their way to the hatter's, 'Rivoli-Deuil' ('deuil' means 'bereavement'), the death masks in the rue Guénégaud, the news on the taxi radio (the daily death toll), the song 'Un Cri d'Amour', the funeral procession that impedes Cléo in *Chapter 7*, the film-within-the-film, the broken pocket mirror, the shooting outside the Dôme café, the Algerian war, and finally, a funeral parlour seen from the bus. Nearly all are filtered through Cléo's subjectivity: we see what she has seen (either via a POV shot or a pan, such as the one that swings round to catch the death masks that make Cléo look so queasy). It is not that Cléo sees real, physical death everywhere (in that sense,

Cléo's antique clock collection and the timer (23.19).

she is not like a pregnant woman, who suddenly notices other pregnant women everywhere), but she appropriates quite innocuous objects or signs and turns them into omens of death. In addition, there are details that we notice as omens of death, which are possibly not noticed by Cléo but that we have become primed to see as symbolic: in Cléo's apartment, near her jewellery, there are four vases filled with *dead* flowers, which seems incongruous in such a tidy and well-kept home. We may also notice many references to time. First and foremost, the chapter titles, as mentioned earlier, constantly remind us of the passage of time. But clocks as physical objects abound in the film: there is a ticking clock at Madame Irma's, which is later confirmed to be the small clock on the mantelpiece showing the correct diegetic time of 5.05; Angèle and Cléo pass a clockmaker on the rue de Rivoli before reaching the taxi rank; there is an odd collection of antique clocks in Cléo's apartment; Cléo uses a small timer for her stretches; we notice street clocks; as she walks in *Chapter 7*, the diegetic sound of her heels segues into the non-diegetic ticking of a clock or a metronome; an ornate clock appears prominently in her flashbacks (showing 3.35); characters are keenly aware of time: José says, 'I haven't the time. Neither have you' as he leaves her; Cléo mentions time twice to Antoine, contradicting herself: 'We have so little time' and later, 'We have all the time in the world.' The motif of the pendulum is also discernible in Cléo's swing, the rocking chair and the swinging camera in *Chapter 6*. This constant and rather terrifying reminder of time is closely associated with a possible impending death, yet it also represents life, time

Street clock, just as radio announces the same time (20.54).

marching on regardless, renewal, rebirth. If the film seems obsessed with death and time, there are also many references to new life, particularly in the second half of the film: the wailing baby in the café in *Chapter 7*; the baby in the incubator seen from the bus and a heavily pregnant woman passing the funeral parlour in *Chapter 13*. In other words, life and death are not separate or opposite entities, but closely entwined and complementary.

Contrary to current and Western conventions, Varda equates death with the colour white, not black: 'When I imagined Cléo in danger, the threat was as white as death. I had read that in oriental countries the colour of bereavement is white.'[72] White is in fact not a colour, but the *absence* of all colour, so it makes sense for white to symbolise the absence of life. White is the dominant 'colour' in *Cléo*, aided of course by the strongest light available, that is to say natural midsummer daylight. The combination of strong sunlight and outdoor scenes, particularly in the wide expanse of the Parc Montsouris, enabled Varda to attain an almost ethereal whiteness in the cinematography. In *Varda par Agnès*, she explains that this effect was created by shooting at dawn using a green filter to counteract the infrared and make the grass appear bleached and 'snowy' (Varda's term).[73] Given that this whiteness is particularly noticeable in the scenes in the park and later again in the Salpêtrière garden, this would seem to point to another instance of nature as hostile and ominous. Yet, I can't help thinking that this is not entirely the case. The whiteness may well represent death or nothingness, but the park – with the Buttes Chaumont, the Parc

Street clock on the Boulevard Raspail (42.14).

Montsouris is one of the more landscaped in Paris – is gorgeous and the camera gracefully glides past its mock waterfalls and down its 'log' staircases so typical of nineteenth-century Parisian garden design. Its brightness and beauty, and the evocative sound of birdsong and tinkling water, create a perfect counterpoint to Cléo's morbidity, just as, in her next film, *Le Bonheur*, Varda would boldly choose to set a disturbing tale of infidelity and death in the most lushly (colour-)photographed countryside. Generally speaking, then, the evocation of death is subtle and subjective in *Cléo*, and some of this subjectivity may well be Varda's.

Nudity and costume, truth and masks

Nudity is undoubtedly one of the key themes in Varda's work and *Cléo de 5 à 7* is no exception. The word itself recurs several times in Varda's introduction to the screenplay, as well as in the dialogue. The summary intended for the Cannes Film Festival states that 'Cléo is a naked young woman embraced by a skeleton and then it's about that young woman's gaze'.[74] This is a little misleading since Cléo herself is never literally naked, and nudity is in fact one of her fears. But this was intended to be taken metaphorically, in the sense that Cléo is at her most vulnerable. The film's trailer goes into more detail regarding Cléo's struggle; a male voiceover sums up the film thus: '[…] it's about a woman caught between questioning and self-discovery, between

Flashback clock (46.53).

coquettishness and angst, between appearance and nudity, thus pitting appearance and surface against nudity and truth.'[75]

Before we turn to the theme of nudity in *Cléo*, it is worth exploring a selection of other examples of nudity in Varda's other films, particularly those that pre-date *Cléo*. In chronological order, the first instance occurs in *L'Opéra-Mouffe* (there is no nudity whatsoever in *La Pointe courte*). This short film is divided into nine sections. In the first segment, entitled 'Des Amoureux', we see, in long shot, a naked couple (Dorothée Blank – already rehearsing for her nude scene in *Cléo* – and José Varéla) emerging from opposite directions into a courtyard where washing is hanging. Later, the naked woman is shown looking at herself in a mirror, with an abstract background of trees. Finally, still in the same segment, but also in the sixth segment, entitled 'Joyeuses Fêtes', we are presented with several shots of the lovers in bed, positioned so as to highlight the abstract quality of their bodies: a close-up of a face (hers), a foot (his) and a hand touching the foot (hers), all in the same frame. I doubt that anyone seeing the film now would find it in any way pornographic, yet at the time, Varda had a great deal of trouble convincing the lab that *L'Opéra-Mouffe* was an art film and not a blue movie. In a hilarious anecdote, Varda recalls how the lab director simply wouldn't believe her and insisted on escorting her to the *bona fide* screening she had booked for her producer and several colleagues.[76] Nudity is certainly seen in a happy and positive light in *L'Opéra-Mouffe*, particularly when it is set against shots of the old and slovenly denizens of the Mouff.

In her documentary about the Côte d'Azur, *Du côté de la côte*, Varda succeeds in inserting a shot of a naked couple after showing us the obligatory serried rows of bikini-clad roasting flesh on the overcrowded beaches of the Riviera. It is obvious that Varda disliked the luxurious and regimented Côte d'Azur and preferred the wilder and less predictable landscapes to the west. After showing us the better-known attractions of the Riviera, Varda 'escapes' by filming a mysterious island, the Eden Roc, which encapsulates her own quest for the Riviera's 'eden'. It is, in complete contrast to the popular beaches, strewn with oiled, but only *semi*-naked, bodies. This tiny island seems deserted. After a lot of previously static shots, Varda lets her camera roam around the unadulterated landscape. Finally, a long track and tilt lead us to a naked couple lying on the beach, an obvious reference to Adam and Eve in this (lost) paradise.

Thus, throughout her career, Varda's nudes may be beautiful but they are never titillating. They are either staged, posed and abstract, or very playful. As a result, and aside from the lab director's brief misreading of *L'Opéra-Mouffe*, Varda never got into trouble with the censors. Sex and nudity had always been commonplace in European cinema, French cinema in particular, and even the iconoclastic New Wave film-makers could not improve on that level of freedom. However, nudity had generally been used as a titillating device to sell films (see, for instance, the opening scene in *Et Dieu… créa la femme/And God Created Woman* (Roger Vadim, 1956), where Brigitte Bardot is shown sunbathing naked on the roof and which Godard subsequently reprised with great irony in the opening post-credit sequence of *Le Mépris*, 1963). The New Wave continued to use sex and nudity to sell films, but in a more original, ironic and 'arty' way (which in Resnais's case bordered on the abstract with *Hiroshima mon amour*, 1959).

By contrast, the nudity in *Cléo de 5 à 7* is brief and not titillating by any means, but it has profound implications. This key theme is not raised before *Chapter 8*, when Cléo visits Dorothée, who is life-modelling in a sculpture school. We discover the school via a subjective tracking shot, which slowly guides us through a room filled with sculptures before entering the second room, where about 20 art students are chipping and hacking at their clay. In the centre of the room, Dorothée is standing, totally naked, with her back turned to the camera/Cléo. All we can hear is the sound of tools on clay. The camera slowly pans and tracks round the room, with some students staring at this obvious intruder, yet no one says a word. When Dorothée is in medium shot, she turns round left, as if she has sensed Cléo's presence behind her, and smiles, obviously pleased to see her. She is not surprised, or embarrassed, yet we know from the conversation that follows that Dorothée has never been seen modelling by Cléo before. As they leave the school, Cléo and Dorothée briefly discuss life-modelling. Dorothée accepts her body and its possible flaws and she is aware of the usefulness of her role. Conversely, Cléo, despite her beauty, is excessively modest and fearful of others' criticism of her potential physical flaws. She mentions this to Antoine in *Chapter 13* and explains that she equates nudity with illness (hospitals) and death, not with life and pleasure. Yet, by broaching this topic with a stranger, she has already begun to bare her soul and this may eventually alter the way she views physical nudity.

In *Cléo de 5 à 7*, the concealment of nudity, costume (designed by Alyette Samazeuilh), has seldom been touched upon, yet it reinforces our perception of the characters and charts Cléo's changing moods and personae in particular. Let us examine Cléo's clothes, accessories, hair and make-up before turning to the other characters in the film.

Cléo has two costume changes: she wears two dresses outdoors and what one could describe as a very flamboyant (in an almost tongue-in-cheek way, but perhaps Cléo is taking it at face value?) négligée, thus providing us with an interesting combination of 'informal' indoor wear and daytime mid-season/summer frocks. By contrast, none of the other characters have costume changes. Three outfits in 90 minutes of narration time may seem a lot, but this is compatible with Cléo's high-maintenance lifestyle and personality. It is also indicative of her restlessness and changeability on that particular afternoon.

In the first four chapters, Cléo wears an ostentatious white dress with large black polka dots. The bodice and skirt are separated by a wide black belt that has a diamond shape at the front, drawing attention to the waist. The dress is sleeveless and as tight as a corset above the waist (in fact Angèle has to 'unlace' her in the café by removing the belt because Cléo has difficulty breathing), but the skirt is more fluid and ample. There is a layering effect with the skirt: a slit in the middle of the ruffled polka-dot top skirt up to the belt reveals a closer-fitting black skirt underneath. Accompanying this excess, Cléo's accessories are mercifully low-key: two-tone court shoes with high stiletto heels, just one bracelet and a ring, and a tiny black purse-like handbag. Her hairdo is busier, however, and is an odd combination of the classic French plait and a 'choucroute' as famously created and worn by Brigitte Bardot, which consisted of piling the hair on top of the head in a 'tidy mess' and pinning it up at the back. It is also oddly stilted and is indeed later revealed to be a wig. We seldom see Cléo in close-up, but her make-up is quite discreet; it emphasises her eyes using eyeliner, which was the classic look of the 1950s and 1960s (see Brigitte Bardot and Audrey Hepburn in particular). The frock itself, with its ample skirt, is reminiscent of the late 1950s and a legacy of the 'New Look' style created after the war by Christian Dior, characterised by a nipped-in waist, prominent breasts, and a very ample long skirt thus exaggerating the hourglass figure. Indeed, Cléo's curves are very much on display in this frock, particularly her breasts, which seem more conical and noticeable than in the more modest black frock later on. In the early 1960s, however, the trend was moving towards a slimmer silhouette and more skinny-looking and close-fitting sheath gowns and pencil skirts as worn by Audrey Hepburn in *Breakfast at Tiffany's* (Blake Edwards, 1961; costumes by Hubert de Givenchy) and Tippy Hedren in *The Birds* (Alfred Hitchcock, 1963; costumes by Edith Head). Indeed there is something rather old-fashioned about Cléo's frock and figure; the large and brash polka dots are by no means tasteful or even trendy.

Cléo changes into her second outfit almost as soon as she returns home in *Chapter 4*. She kicks off her shoes immediately and puts on some flat white satin slippers. In long shot, we see her removing her polka-dot dress, briefly revealing a 'Maidenform' short white slip.[77] While she stretches her body at the bar, Angèle helps her into an ample and long white satin brocade négligée trimmed at the collar and sleeves with ostrich feather, and with additional white fabric roses at the collar. At the back, there is a wide panel of fabric that becomes a train. It is a rather ludicrous accoutrement, halfway between an eighteenth-century female gown as featured in Watteau's paintings, and a Japanese geisha's kimono (though not as colourful). It is at once utterly impractical (the ostrich trim in particular, but also the train that hampers her movements and which the kittens like to play with) and modest (it covers Cléo from ankle to neck, though the boat neckline does reveal part of the shoulders and the top of her back). This said, it is quite graceful, particularly because of the ostrich feathers that replicate Cléo's every move, though in slow motion. It works particularly well with sinuous camera movements and the long-focus lens that softens the image. On the other hand, it seems an incongruous outfit in such a modern and artistic (in the Montparnasse artists' studio tradition) loft space, which evokes more Andy Warhol's Factory than the French eighteenth century of Marivaux or Beaumarchais.

Finally, when Cléo decides to storm out of the rehearsal, she changes into a radically different sober black dress, which lends her infinitely more gravitas. 'I'll wear black. It goes with your songs,' she petulantly exclaims as she emerges from behind the black curtain-cum-screen. The frock is sleeveless and close-fitting with an unusual gored skirt with flared panels in a lighter-shade print. As would have been expected at the time, the dress has a matching stole and square handbag, both in the same lighter fabric as the dress, though the stole is black on one side. Cléo wears lighter shoes with a lower heel, and decides to wear a necklace this time, presumably to lighten the severity of the frock's bodice. The unusual, exotic (Latin American?) and 'Left Bank'-style[78] necklace was apparently Varda's own and has a large, though not ostentatious, pendant.[79] All in all, Cléo's third and final outfit is the epitome of sobriety and good taste (particularly once she has discarded the 'ridiculous' black hat purchased earlier at the hatter's): she looks slimmer, less of a Barbie doll/sex bomb, yet she has retained a certain movement and playfulness with the flared skirt. This said, even in black, Corinne Marchand's figure is still more 'womanly' than other New Wave actresses. In the Dôme café, she wears the typical 1960s dark glasses, which were quite pointed at the top corners. Last but not least, she has removed her beehive wig, not to reveal darker hair, as we might have expected, but the exact same shade of platinum blonde hair, though in a straight, short and sober bob. Her make-up remains unchanged.

It is clear that these three outfits chart three different facets of Cléo's personality as well as three stages of the narration: the living doll who is partly fake (the wig, but one may also wonder to what extent her bosom is enhanced by padding) and an exhibitionist; the woman whose indoor clothing/cloak conveys that she never relaxes and is never totally 'herself', but is always ready to receive guests and act a part (mistress, performer, etc.); the more genuine Cléo/Florence, a woman who is subtly elegant and able to blend in with rather than stand out from the crowd. This final outfit is strongly reminiscent of the nineteenth-century *flâneur*; someone who did not want to be seen, let alone recognised, who dressed very soberly, usually in black, unlike the dandy, to whom the *flâneur* has been likened, yet who preferred to be noticed and admired in colourful raiment, like Beau Brummell: '[B]lack […] makes man and his surroundings equal – a state which would be intolerable for the dandy (who needs to be seen), but advantageous to the *flâneur* who wanders through the city "in order to find the things which will occupy his gaze and thus complete his otherwise incomplete identity".[80] Indeed, in the black dress, Cléo does become anonymous and is thus better able to observe others and leave aside her former 'fake' identity.

All the other characters in the film, by contrast, are more ordinary in their costumes. Perhaps the only exception is Antoine, because he wears a uniform (though this is not apparent at first because he is carrying his jacket and is not wearing his hat). Somehow, Antoine wears the uniform as if to indicate that it does not possess him; it seems to glide off him. As a result, we can easily picture him in civilian dress. This is partly because he does not draw attention to it, but also because a military uniform in a park seems so incongruous: war in the midst of peaceful nature. Of course, at the time it wouldn't have seemed that odd since soldiers were ubiquitous in the days of general conscription and long military service. On the other hand, we can't imagine José in anything but the very dapper light grey suit that he wears when visiting Cléo. Angèle is reminiscent of a duenna, always in black, though with a pattern (the zebra pattern on the front of her top for instance). She is elegantly dressed, in a sort of sober housekeeper's uniform. Finally, Dorothée's summer dress is easy to wear and simple, hassle-free. It is sleeveless and only slightly fitted, with an abstract pattern of vertical stripes. One can't imagine her in a corset-like frock, in fact, unlike Cléo, she is not wearing a slip, nor even a bra. Her hair is loose and wavy, with just a hair band to keep it off her face. She is naturally pretty, without excessive or even noticeable grooming.

One no doubt feels tempted to view Cléo's first two outfits as an expression of her fakeness, in contrast to the final outfit, which would appear to represent the 'real' Cléo. In the first half of the film, she seems to be wearing a mask (symbolically represented, at one remove, by the wig, not by heavy make-up), whereas her demeanour in the second half seems less forced and more genuine, no doubt in accordance with her more sober attire. Yet, perhaps Cléo's initial overt 'fakeness' signifies merely a different facet of her persona (i.e. the pop star), rather than a less genuine one. Cléo, with her blondeness, her curves and her spoilt behaviour, plays the role of the ultimate seductress. According to Baudrillard, the seductress draws attention to her own fakeness and therefore becomes a figure of innocence.[81] Just as, according to Nietzsche, art that foregrounds its artificiality and does not wish to deceive is superior because it is more true.[82] In other words, Cléo is genuine in her display of a masquerade. Furthermore, we may like to think that Cléo's 'fakeness' is imposed on her by patriarchy, yet simultaneously, the men in the film belittle and criticise her (Bob and José in particular) precisely on the grounds of her appearance. Indeed, some feminists have denounced patriarchy for imposing behaviour or values on women (they must be on display and attractive at all times) and then proceeding to dismiss these same women as frivolous. Varda points this out in a subtle way, and to a certain extent, indicts us, the spectators, for falling into the knee-jerk pitfall of initially judging Cléo by her doll-like appearance.

Costume is consequently not just a means of making *Cléo de 5 à 7* a more stylish and enjoyable film; it also carries symbolic meaning, particularly in relation to the motif of nudity, which is presented as something Cléo lacks and needs. Costume also highlights the contrast between Cléo and her environment; the 'real' people in the streets wear 'real' clothes, whereas Cléo's clothes, even her final 'camouflage' outfit, are a costume, a masquerade to protect her against the reality of the outside world.

Cléo de 5 à 7's clever illusion of 'real' time, its complex *mise-en-scène*, its debt to literature and its thematic richness endow the film with both modernity and perennity. Thematically, *Cléo* illustrates several of Varda's *auteurist* traits: subjectivity, mortality, fate, nudity and human interaction as a means to self-awareness and maturity. In the next chapter, I will examine how the film was received on its release both at home and abroad and how it is still generating discussion and analysis.

Notes

1   Konigsberg, Ira, *The Complete Film Dictionary* (London: Bloomsbury, 1993), p. 378.

2   TV has also attempted real-time narration with the series *24*, in which 24 episodes recount 24 hours, though each episode is actually 40 minutes long to allow for commercial breaks.

3   Kawin, Bruce F., *How Movies Work* (New York: Macmillan, 1987), p. 59.

4   Bordwell, David, *Narration in the Fiction Film* (London: Routledge, 1985), p. 49.

5   Claudia Gorbman mistakenly believed that this was a temporal ambiguity and was mystified by a whole 30 minutes being unaccounted for (Gorbman, Claudia,

'*Cleo from 5 to 7*: music as mirror', *Wide Angle* 4.4, 1981, p. 41). In fact, the film's theatrical trailer clearly specifies that there is no ambiguity and that the plot/story time is from 5 to 6.30, despite the title. A male voiceover announces: 'Cleo from 5 to 7, *or rather from 5 to 6.30*, is about a woman caught between questioning and self-discovery, between coquettishness and angst, between appearance and nudity' (my italics).

6   I am using Edward Branigan's sophisticated definition here: 'The POV shot is a shot in which the camera assumes the position of a subject in order to show us what the subject sees.' Branigan in fact breaks the POV shot down into two distinct shots: the point/glance shot (a shot of a character looking off-screen) and the point/object shot (a shot of what that character was looking at in the previous shot). See Branigan, Edward, *Point of View in The Cinema: A Theory of Narration and Subjectivity in Classical Film* (Berlin: Mouton, 1984), p. 103.

7   Bordwell: *Narration in the Fiction Film*, p. 83.

8   Nicolas Boileau, *L'Art poétique* (1674).

9   Isidore Isou (1928–). A Romanian-born artist working in Pari who was the founder of the Lettriste movement associated with the Situationist branch (headed by Guy Debord) of the Anarchist movement. Isou made just one film, *Traité de bave et d'éternité/Venom and Eternity*, in 1950. The most immediately striking feature of Lettrisme is its extensive use of words and letters. Words can appear unexpectedly, sometimes painted directly onto film stock then projected in a cinema, thus subverting the photographic realism of film and turning it into a form of visual poetry.

10 For convenience, I am referring to the institutional mode of representation as defined by Noël Burch in *The Theory of Film Practice* (1969) (London: Secker and Warburg, 1973). In film, the IMR is a set of codes and conventions of *mise-en-scène*, framing and (continuity) editing contributing to spatio-temporal coherence that engages, yet is imperceptible to, the spectator.

11 Cook, Pam (ed.), *The Cinema Book* (London: BFI, 1985), p. 212.

12 Varda: *Varda par Agnès*, p. 236.

13 Hitchcock explains the MacGuffin in detail in his book-length interview with François Truffaut, *Hitchcock by Truffaut: The Definitive Study* (London: Paladin, 1986), pp. 191–195. The MacGuffin appears typically as spy papers or plans (*The Thirty-nine Steps*, 1935), a sample of uranium in a wine bottle (*Notorious*, 1946) or a case of seriously mistaken identity (*North by Northwest*, 1959).

14 Varda: *Cléo de 5 à 7*, The centrefold.

15 Uytterhoeven, Pierre, 'Agnès Varda, de 5 à 7', *Positif* 44, March 1962, p. 14.

16 Anthony, Elizabeth M., 'From fauna to flora in Agnès Varda's *Cléo de 5 à 7*', *Literature/Film Quarterly* 26.2, 1998, p. 93.

17 Uytterhoeven: 'Agnès Varda de 5 à 7', p. 3.

18 Varda: *Cléo*, p. 8. '[…] les chapitres ont des noms de personnes, ils colorent le récit, ou plutôt l'angle sous lequel est peint le portrait de Cléo.'

19 Konigsberg: *The Complete Film Dictionary*, p. 187.

20 Varda: *Cléo*, p. 8.

21 Varda: *Cléo*, p. 67.

22 Varda: *Cléo*, p. 47. 'Séquence à la va-comme-je-te-pousse […].'

23 Varda: *Cléo*, p. 89. 'Le chapitre sera filmé en un seul plan, comme une respiration profonde.' It is sometimes difficult to translate 'respiration' in the context of film editing. One could also use 'pulse'. Agnès Guillemot, Godard's long-standing

editor, argues that Godard does not so much specialise in jump cuts 'as in cinema's correct pulse [*respiration*]'. Quoted in Thierry Jousse and Frédéric Strauss, 'Entretien avec Agnès Guillemot', *Cahiers du cinéma*, 10 August 1991, p. 61.

24 Tailleur, Roger, 'Cléo d'ici à l'éternité', *Positif*, 44 March 1962, p. 18.

25 Gorbman: '*Cléo from 5 to 7*: music as mirror', pp. 38–49.

26 Gorbman: '*Clèo from 5 to 7*: music as mirror', pp. 43–44.

27 Gorbman: '*Clèo from 5 to 7*: music as mirror', p. 48.

28 Bogart: *Music and Narrative in the French New Wave: The Films of Agnès Varda and Jacques Demy*, p. 220.

29 Bogart: *Music and Narrative in the French New Wave*, p. 220.

30 Vincendeau, Ginette, *Stars and Stardom in French Cinema* (London: Continuum, 2000), p. 117.

31 Vincendeau: *Stars and Stardom in French Cinema*, p. 118.

32 Flitterman-Lewis: *To Desire Differently: Feminism and the French Cinema*, p. 223.

33 Varda: *Cléo*, p. 23. '[…] soubrette – marraine – confidente, un peu maquerelle, un peu tata.'

34 Interestingly, Irma is being quite euphemistic here. The Queen of Spades in fact represents one of the most evil females in the deck: 'A dark woman, probably a widow or a divorcee. She is extremely unpleasant and will bring trouble to anyone who comes into close contact with her.' Miller, Carey, *The Target Book of Fate and Fortune* (London: W.H. Allen, 1977), p. 80.

35 The 'Hand of Fatima' is a Muslim amulet with only a very tenuous link to Fatima, the devoted daughter of the prophet Muhammad, and who is a sacred female figure in Islam. According to lore, this amulet is supposed to ward off the 'evil eye' and protect from danger, sickness and bad luck.

36 Darche, Claude, *Initiation pratique au tarot: Tirages et interprétations divinatoires à la portée de tous* (St-Jean-de-Braye: Dangles, 1992), p. 80.

37 Varda: *Cléo*, p. 15.

38 *Sex and the City*, season 1, episode 12, 'Oh Come All Ye Faithful' (HBO, 1998).

39 Fein, Ellen, and Sherrie Schneider, *The Rules: Time-Tested Secrets for Capturing the Heart of Mr Right* (London: Harper Collins, 1995).

40 Uytterhoeven: 'Agnès Varda de 5 à 7', p. 8.

41 Levitin: 'Mother of the New Wave: An Interview with Agnès Varda', p. 64.

42 Darche: *Initiation pratique au tarot*, p. 21.

43 Utilitarianism is a doctrine in ethics, which argues that an action is right if it tends to promote happiness and wrong if it tends to produce the reverse of happiness – not just the happiness of the performer of the action but also that of everyone affected by it. See also Falzon, Christopher, *Philosophy Goes to the Movies: An Introduction to Philosophy* (London: Routledge, 2002), p. 109.

44 Michel Marie, David Bordwell, Richard Neupert, Dudley Andrew, etc.

45 Sterrit, David, *The Films of Jean-Luc Godard: Seeing the Invisible* (New York: Cambridge University Press, 1999), pp. 56–60.

46 Sartre, Jean-Paul, *Being and Nothingness: An Essay on Phenomenological Ontology*, trans. Hazel E. Barnes (London: Methuen, 1957), p. 59.

47 Sartre: *Being and Nothingness*, p. 59.

48 Sartre: *Being and Nothingness*, p. 60.

49 Varda: *Cléo*, p. 34.

50 Varda: *Cléo*, p. 64.

51 Stephen Spender, introduction to Rilke, Rainer, Maria, *The Notebook of Malte Laurids Brigge,* trans. John Lindon (Oxford: Oxford University Press, 1984), p. xv.

52 Jean-Paul Sartre, *Huis clos* (Paris: Folio/Gallimard, 1975), p. 44.

53 'Se promener sans hâte, au hasard, en s'abandonnant à l'impression et au spectacle du moment.' Dictionnaire Petit Robert 1, 1986 edition.

54 Collins Dictionary, 1994 edition.

55 Max Ophüls (1902–1957) was a German director famed, in part, for his over-wrought visual style using extremely graceful and intricate camera movements.

56 Carné, Marcel, 'Quand le cinéma descendra-t-il dans la rue?', *Cinémagazine,* November 1933.

57 Gleber, Anke, *The Art of Taking a Walk: Flânerie, Literature and Film in Weimar Culture* (Princeton, NJ: Princeton University Press, 1999), p. 7.

58 Fournel, Victor, *Ce qu'on voit dans les rues de Paris* (Paris: Adolphe Delahays, 1858).

59 Benjamin, Walter, *The Arcades Project,* trans. Howard Eiland and Kevin McLaughlin (Cambridge, Mass.: Harvard University Press, 1999).

60 Buck-Morss, Susan, 'The flâneur, the sandwichman and the whore: the Politics of loitering', *New German Critique* 39, Autumn 1986, pp. 99–140.

61 Friedberg, Anne, *Window Shopping: Cinema and the Postmodern* (Berkeley: University of California Press, 1993), p. 35.

62 Mouton, Janice, 'From feminine masquerade to flâneuse: Agnès Varda's Cléo in the city', *Cinema Journal* 40.2, Winter 2001, p. 7.

63 Quoted in Ariane Litaize, '*Cléo de 5 à 7*': Fiche Filmographique IDHEC no. 187, 1 January 1962, p. 3.

64 Woolf, Virginia, *Mrs Dalloway* (London: Wordsworth Classics, 1996), p. 5.

65 Woolf: *Mrs Dalloway* p. 8.

66 Puaux, Françoise, 'Paris vu par Agnès Varda: une glaneuse des villes', http://www.forumdesimages.net/fr/alacarte/htm/LEPARISDE/VARDA/VARD A.htm, p. 1. Accessed April 2005.

67 Brassaï (1899–1984) was a Hungarian-born poet, draftsman, sculptor and photographer known primarily for his dramatic and sometimes sleazy photographs of Paris at night.

68 Robert Doisneau (1912–1994), captured the lives of ordinary people doing ordinary things in post-war Paris; Henri Cartier-Bresson (1908–2004) was a French photographer whose spontaneous photographs helped establish photo-journalism as an art form.

69 Puaux: 'Paris vu par Agnès Varda: une glaneuse des villes', p. 1.

70 Puaux, 'Paris vu par Agnès Varda: une glaneuse des villes', p. 3.

71 Varda: *Agnès*, p. 70.

72 Varda: *Agnès*, p. 62.

73 Varda: *Agnès*, p.62.

74 Varda: *Cléo*, p. 10.

75 Varda: *Cléo*, p. 10.

76 Varda: *Agnès*, p. 115.

77 Maidenform is an American ladies' underwear manufacturer that used to specialise in underwear designed to contain the female form while enhancing the breasts with padding. Thus the waist was nipped in, the thighs slimmed down but the breasts prominent and jutting out.

78   There are many shops on the Left Bank selling this sort of ethnic jewellery, as opposed to the glamorous rocks of the Right Bank's Place Vendôme.

79   Mounier, Monique, 'Agnès Varda: "le cinéma n'est pas plus difficile pour une femme que pour un homme"', *Paris-Presse*, 17 April 1962.

80   Ponikwer, Fiona, *Communicating with the (Un-)dead: A Study of Vampirism as Self-renewal in France – 1850–1900*, p. 16. Unpublished doctoral thesis, University of East Anglia, 1998.

81   Baudrillard, Jean, *Seduction*, trans. B. Singer (London: Macmillan Education, 1990), p. 94. Cited in Catherine Constable, 'Making up the truth: on lies, lipstick and Friedrich Nietzsche', in Stella Bruzzi and Pamela Church-Gibson (eds), *Fashion Cultures: Theories, Explorations and Analysis* (London: Routledge, 2000), p. 197.

82   Brezeale, D. (ed. and trans.), *Philosophy and Truth: Selections from Nietzsche's Notebooks of the Early 1870s* (Atlantic Highlands, NJ and London: Humanities Press International, 1979), p. 96. Quoted in Constable, 'Making up the truth', p. 197.

3 Reception

Box office and reviews

Despite the fact that the New Wave was still in full swing, 1962 was not a boom year in French cinema: only 90 films (either French or French co-productions) were released. Compared to the outstanding vintage of 1960 (124 films, many of which were first films by young directors), or even 1957 (111), French cinema seemed to be on the wane. *Cléo de 5 à 7* was released on 11 April 1962 and was included in the Cannes Film Festival's official selection in May 1962. It went on to be selected for the Venice Film Festival in September that year. Although the film did not win anything at either festival, it obtained the Prix Méliès in 1963.[1] Box office takings were very respectable: 553,545 admissions in total for the 1961–1962 season. By comparison, the French blockbuster for that year was the comedy *La Guerre des boutons/The War of the Buttons* (Yves Robert, 1962), with 9.8 million spectators. However, if we compare *Cléo* with the New Wave output of that year, it did less well than Alain Resnais's *L'Année dernière à Marienbad* (882,148) and Truffaut's *Jules et Jim* (1.5 million).[2] However, judging by the comments in the French press, the film was the must-see event of April 1962.[3] This said, some critics were quite prophetic in their belief that *Cléo de 5 à 7* was not just a flash in the pan but would also stand the test of time: '[…] a film which will become a cine-club classic,' thought a *Canard Enchaîné* reviewer.[4]

In France, reviews were generally positive, if not ecstatic in some cases. The cinephile film journal *Positif*, which had lambasted Godard's films for being immature and sloppy, had far more respect for non-*Cahiers* New Wave directors such as Demy, Resnais, Marker and, of course, Varda. The March 1962 issue (no. 44) had *Cléo de 5 à 7* on the cover, a still from the scene where

Cléo is enquiring after her results at the reception of the Salpêtrière hospital. The issue begins with an informative 14-page interview with Varda followed by a long and extraordinarily detailed review by Roger Tailleur. Tailleur clearly adored the film: the review is brimming with superlatives and he praises Varda's blend of contradictions in particular. *Cléo de 5 à 7* also featured on the cover of *Cahiers du cinéma* of April 1962 (but this time, it is when she is trying on a black-veiled creation at the hatter's).[5] The review by Claude Beylie, entitled 'Le Triomphe de la femme', is long and favourable, but not as detailed as Tailleur's and focuses largely on the 'femininity' of the film.[6] The February 1963 issue of *Cahiers du cinéma* featured the top ten lists for 1962 of 38 film writers and critics (all male), 12 of whom cited *Cléo de 5 à 7*. Interestingly, even though Jean-Luc Godard played in the film and had previously greatly admired Varda's shorts,[7] he did not include *Cléo* in his top ten films of 1962.

Naturally enough, virtually every review remarked upon the gender of *Cléo*'s creator. Indeed, Varda was almost the only female director in France in the 1960s. Before her there had been Alice Guy-Blaché (1873–1968), Germaine Dulac (1882–1942), Marie Epstein (1899–1995) and Jacqueline Audry (1908–1977, mostly active during the 1950s) and there would be many more after her, but she was the only woman making New Wave films in the 1950s and 1960s.[8] Many reviews also noted, like Tailleur, that Varda hadn't made life easy for herself by choosing to tell a story in real time.[9] Her ambitiousness was praised, even though some thought the film overly verbose[10] and her visual style a tad gimmicky. Claude Mauriac, writing for *Le Figaro Littéraire* (14 April 1962), thought the film, and the script in particular, was too polished. He would have preferred more documentary realism and deplored the fact that the Dôme café patrons were not in fact real people but extras who had learned their lines. For Mauriac, it was too obvious that these (to my mind) wonderfully poetic snatches of conversation (quite similar, in fact, to the more surreal snippets in *L'Année dernière à Marienbad*) had previously been written by Varda and were not authentic. In effect, Mauriac wanted or expected a documentary, yet Varda claimed to have wanted to make a subjective documentary, 'subjective' being the operative word here: *Cléo de 5 à 7* is first and foremost a fiction film, though with documentary-*like* aspects.

Finally, if many critics agreed that Varda's film was 'intelligent', then nearly all of them were rather derogatory regarding Cléo's character (i.e. not Corinne Marchand's acting). The fact that they considered her a pea-brained *sotte* ('fool') undermined the film in their opinion. The anonymous reviewer in *Démocratie* (19 April 1962) compares *Cléo de 5 à 7* to Bergman's *Wild Strawberries*, yet argues that the former is inferior because '[t]he analysis of Cléo's soul-searching is inevitably more limited given that she is a fool'. Varda has never referred to Cléo as a 'fool'. Although she does not feel any real affection towards Cléo, she has admitted to feeling sorry for her heroine, because 'I think that it's awful for someone to have to think about death when they're not prepared for it'.[11] Indeed, would the film have had the same poignancy if Cléo had been an older, more mature and stoic character? And what does intelligence have to do with the fear of death anyway?

Interestingly, not many reviewers or critics have commented on the film-within-the-film. Some disliked it; for Roy Armes it is 'very unfunny'.[12] Varda herself later reappraised it: 'I don't like the impression it gives of a "private joke".'[13] The film is merely a distraction for Cléo and does not appear to have a deep or hidden symbolic meaning besides warning the viewer against pessimism and overdramatisation. It strongly exemplifies New Wave trends by citing and affectionately lampooning silent cinema and is indeed very much an in-joke. From a narrative point of view, it makes us aware of Cléo's (off-screen) subjectivity: she succeeds in briefly forgetting about her worries (as do we) by immersing herself in another's unfounded grief.

Turning now to British and American reviews, again, most were favourable, such as Richard Roud's in *Sight and Sound* (no. 31, Summer 1962).[14] Roud was particularly impressed by the way Varda 'has beautifully struck a balance between the frivolity of Cléo's little group and the outside world – the streets of Paris, its shops and parks'. Foreign reviewers may have been more sensitive to and more excited about the realist representation of Paris, unlike French reviewers, who were occasionally 'bored' by this Paris that was overly familiar to them. For instance, Henri Chapier admitted in *Combat* that the bus ride felt 'interminable' to him. Some French reviewers, however, thought Paris was shot from a different perspective: 'A Paris that is familiar yet seems like another planet.'[15] Like some French critics, Bosley Crowther, writing for the *New York Times* (5 September 1962), admired the *mise-en-scène*, but also believed that 'Varda is so absorbed with her camera stunts [...] that the essential concentration on the heroine is neglected and the interest lost'. Crowther is not more explicit about these 'stunts', but I imagine that he is referring to the changes in focalisation from chapter to chapter and particularly the 'swinging' camera in *Chapter 6*, and possibly also the 'flashes'. Interestingly, more recent reviews of the film (for TV transmissions or Varda retrospectives) do not dwell on the *mise-en-scène* or its potentially 'irritating' quality. This is a classic example of filmic style whose novelty may have irritated at first but later became unobtrusive because it was no longer new or unique. 'MTV-style editing' is a good example of this. It also demonstrates two things: Varda's style was groundbreaking in 1962, yet at the same time, her film has succeeded in ageing well. However, even though her style is no longer considered overwrought and annoying, her character still is. Furthermore, Crowther et al omitted to mention that certain sequences in *Cléo de 5 à 7* are extraordinarily simple and straightforward, such as *Chapter 12*, for instance, through Antoine's focalisation, filmed in one long take (unless one considers the long take to be a 'stunt').

Finally, although very few loathed the film, one review stands out in particular, mostly for its lampooning of New Wave practices, by Stanley Kauffman in *A World on Film* (1966):

> How Do You Know You Can't Be a New-Wave Director? Have you tried? Follow these simple steps […] 1. Get a good cameraman. 2. Get a story. Your story need not be gripping or valid. 3. Cast the female lead with a photogenic girl. 4. Lay it on. 'It' is the New Wave repertoire of stunts, camera techniques and cutting. Examples: use freakish faces for minor characters (this is candor). Use a little nudeness (this is maturity). Include long walks through a city, preferably Paris; just long, pointless walks – to show that you are as free of plot contrivances as Antonioni. Dwell on such *bizarrerie* as street performers who swallow and regurgitate live frogs or who push hatpins through their biceps (this shows how ugly life is and how you are facing it). Let your microphone record snatches of irrelevant conversations at neighboring café tables (this wraps your story in a naturalistic web). Retain the footage where passers-by stare into the camera (thus you prove that you 'stole' your film from the street and that you wear your *rue* with a difference). Do not omit Resnais backward jumps (cutting back to a moment just passed) as this expresses a mystique about time. Have your heroine sing a torch song, Judy Garlanded with *Angst*.[16]

If this weren't enough, Kauffman thought *Cléo de 5 à 7* was 'an over-sentimental, overly imitative, soap-opera-like soupy tale'.[17] Beyond the superficially amusing quality of the sheer viciousness of Kauffman's appraisal, it is difficult to seriously consider his view because he is merely articulating what he personally dislikes about the New Wave. On the other hand, Kauffman is quite accurate: most New Wave films were 'guilty' of most, if not all, of the above, and *Cléo* was no exception. But whether these were weaknesses or a much-needed breath of fresh air in French cinema is a matter of opinion. However, it is hard to agree with Kauffman's final comment: one could not possibly accuse Varda of being over-sentimental, even though the topic has tear-jerker potential; nor could one seriously consider the film in any way derivative (Kauffman does not go into more detail). Finally, Kauffman is presumably referring to the unity of time or its 'femininity' when he calls it 'soap-opera-like', though again, this is not entirely clear. A soap opera would certainly have more interwoven storylines and cliffhangers. Surely it would begin, rather than end, with Cléo's diagnosis and prognosis, or it would certainly end in resolution, either tragic or 'happy'.

On that subject, critics and scholars have had much to say. Many French reviewers used the word *condamnée* ('doomed') to describe Cléo's fate. Of course, nothing is less certain, and Varda herself refused to give anything away in the script, where she ambiguously stated that Cléo was '*probably* destined for death' (my italics).[18] Others acknowledged the ambiguity; Aubriant refers to all the omens that seem to point to death, and yet they are omens that spectators do not necessarily believe in, and which may well be so many red herrings.[19] Similarly, Jean de Baroncelli in *Le Monde* (23 April 1962) argues that the film is *about* uncertainty and the wait, and not the result. As I mentioned in Chapter Two, Cléo's future, or lack of one, is the MacGuffin, and is consequently immaterial to us. Serge Daney's response ('unimportant') is the correct one. On the other hand, I have always wondered how *Cléo* succeeds in being such a feel-good film despite its subject matter. Despite having been aligned with Cléo's point of view, despite becoming close to her during these 90 minutes, her relief and happiness, odd though it may seem, are palpable in the closing sequence.[20]

In film, there is what I would bluntly call 'the fatal illness genre', or even more specifically, 'the terminal cancer genre', for cancer is generally the fatal illness in question at least before AIDS. There are a number of films on this theme, often focusing on female characters, though only occasionally made by female directors. It is debatable whether *Cléo de 5 à 7* falls into this category since it is not certain that her cancer is terminal, and moreover, the film ends, rather than begins with, her diagnosis. Admittedly, some 'terminal cancer films' do not begin with a diagnosis (e.g. *Terms of Endearment*, James L. Brooks, 1983), but the cancer is generally advanced by the film's second half.

One recent 'terminal cancer film' is both similar and very different to *Cléo*. Isabel Coixet's *My Life Without Me* (2003) starring Sarah Polley as Ann, the 'me' of the title, begins typically with the announcement of Ann's terminal ovarian cancer. Ironically, her cancer is untreatable because of her young age (23), which means it is more aggressive. She is told she has only a couple of months to live. A wife and mother of two, Ann tells no one but pragmatically writes a list of the ten things she feels she must do before she dies. The film charts her last few months, in which she achieves all but one of her goals. Half of these ten goals focus on others ('Find Don [her husband] a new wife who the girls like'), the other five centre on her and her desire to do things that she's never had time or inclination to do before ('Smoke and drink as much as I want'; 'Make love with other men to see what it is like'). The film opens with a series of handheld close-ups of Ann standing in the rain with her eyes closed, in daylight. Her voice in interior monologue informs us that she has never done anything like this before: 'This is you. Eyes closed, out in the rain. You never thought you'd be doing something like this.' Cléo also behaves out of character when she storms out after the rehearsal and wanders around her neighbourhood, observing people, listening, as if for the first time. The expression 'out of character' is important here. Both characters are behaving 'abnormally', that is to say against their own norms: Cléo only paid attention to herself, she was literally 'self-conscious'; Ann didn't have time to pay any attention to herself, her thoughts and time were always for others. When she collapses and is taken to hospital, she obsessively asks the nurses and doctors if someone has informed her mother so that her daughters can be picked up from school. Ann, as her name partly indicates, is quite ordinary and average. Indeed, she is quite 'normal' even though she tells her mother there's no such thing. Cléo, on the other hand, bears a name that is not her own, since her real name is Florence. It's a fantasy, a mask, evocative of ancient Egypt, of goddesses, of exceptional women. Whereas Ann will strive to be less ordinary by planning her remaining months in this extraordinary way, Cléo will attempt to be more 'normal', walking in the street, listening to people, taking the bus.

Objectively, one could argue that Ann has very little: she works as a night cleaner and lives in a trailer. Yet, despite the fact that she possesses nothing *material*, she has everything else: a husband she loves, a family (even if her mother often annoys her and her father is in jail) and friends. Cléo is the exact opposite: she has all the material trappings (a successful pop career, a nice home, a maid/confidante, a rich older lover – if the last two can be considered 'material'!) but she's lonely in her time of need. She does have a friend in the character of Dorothée, though she remembers her only when she needs her, and Dorothée, although sympathetic to Cléo's predicament, cannot really help her. Significantly, there is no mention of a family. Angèle seems to have become a surrogate mother. One of the major themes in the film is Cléo's fear of nudity (because linked to death, birth, hospitals). Ann, on the other hand, is a very *naked* person (and, cleverly, the director never shows her naked on-screen). Yet, she does not consider herself naked enough; one of her must-do items is to 'say what [she's] thinking'.

Besides the theme of death, the subject that stimulated reviewers most in *Cléo de 5 à 7* was love. As I mentioned in Chapter Two, Varda was dismissive of those critics who believed Cléo and Antoine's relationship was one of burgeoning love. Through body language and dialogue, the film hints that this will remain a platonic and brotherly friendship. On the other hand, one reviewer believed that Cléo and Dorothée could in fact be more than just friends: 'The final long shot of Dorothée as Cléo watches her climb an outdoor stairway is accompanied in the music track by the piano accompaniment for the song "Cri d'Amour", suggesting perhaps a depth of feeling between the two woman [sic] that the film chooses further not to explore.'[21] While I would agree that the soundtrack adds poignancy to Dorothée's ascent of the stairs, it never occurred to me that this could be for romantic reasons. I would be more inclined to interpret this as Cléo's internal 'melodrama', her feeling that she may not see Dorothée again, or for some time.

A feminist film?

Even though Agnès Varda may not consciously have made feminist films, or at least, not until later in her career, some scholars and critics acknowledged the feminist legacy of her films from the outset. This said, and as Susan Hayward has rightly observed, 'Varda's work is often passed over in silence in anthologies on women's film – and yet she herself claims to be an avowed feminist.'[22] For example, there is only one mention of Varda (regarding art cinema) in Annette Kuhn's *Women's Pictures* and none at all in Alison Butler's more recent *Women's Cinema: The Contested Screen*.[23] On the other hand, quite a few studies on female directors do devote whole sections to Varda, for instance Jeanne Betancourt's *Women in Focus*,[24] Louise Heck-Rabi's *Women Filmmakers: A Critical Reception*,[25] Barbara Koenig Quart's *Women Directors: The Emergence of a New Cinema*,[26] the entry in Annette Kuhn and Susannah Radstone (eds), *The Women's Companion to International Film*[27] and Ally Acker's *Reel Women: Pioneers of the Cinema 1896 to the Present*.[28] Generally speaking, English-language books that feature sections on Varda tend to focus on gender issues, whereas studies in French (for instance Siclier or Bazin)[29] are far more interested in Varda's obvious status as *auteur*. Sandy Flitterman-Lewis, and later Alison Smith, consider both gender and *auteurism* in their work on Varda.[30]

Reviewed chronologically, the feminist interpretation of *Cléo de 5 à 7* reveals fluctuations representative of different feminist eras, ranging from the 'puritanical' feminism of the 1970s to the more tempered post-feminist reading of the 1990s, which championed the feminist discourse of the film, reverting to a more questioning view in the new millennium. In the early days of feminist film criticism, there was some dissent, with a few feminist scholars being frustrated by what they perceived as a reactionary and essentialist conception of femininity present in Varda's work. Claire Johnstone, in her seminal 1976 essay 'Women's Cinema as Counter-Cinema', was disappointed in Varda's films, and *Le Bonheur* – probably Varda's most misunderstood film from a feminist standpoint – in particular: 'The films of Agnès Varda are a particularly good example of an œuvre which celebrates bourgeois myths of women, and with it the apparent innocence of the sign.'[31] She goes on to criticise Varda's essentialism, namely the association of femininity with the biological, the natural and the physical, which removes women from any kind of historical evolution – the myth of the 'eternal feminine': 'There is no doubt that Varda's work is reactionary: in her rejection of culture and her placement of woman outside history, her films mark a retrograde step in women's cinema.'[32] It is true that essentialism goes against the grain of traditional feminist thought epitomised in Simone de Beauvoir's celebrated phrase 'on ne naît pas femme, on le devient',[33] 'one is not born, but rather becomes, a woman', in *The Second Sex* (1949) – her plea for the abolition of the myth of the 'eternal feminine', resulting in education, culture and history transcending a mere biological given. Essentialism is certainly present in *L'Opéra-Mouffe*, which centres on the pregnant body, and *Réponse de femmes* (1975), a critique of how women's bodies are portrayed, treated and perceived in society and the media, but there is little evidence of essentialism in *Cléo de 5 à 7*, a film that Johnstone does not in fact mention at all. Cléo briefly and discreetly mentions to Dorothée that her cancer is 'dans le ventre', which could be translated either as 'stomach' or 'womb', and so makes only a fleeting and ambiguous reference to her specifically gendered physical dimension.

What some feminist critics resented about *Cléo* was that her character barely seemed to change over the course of the film. Cléo was not sufficiently aware and remained merely a pretty object. Françoise Audé, for example, wrote that '[s]he moves a short way from the status of desirable object to that of subject, but it is a movement which is hardly perceptible.'[34] For Audé, the 90-minute diegesis was just too short to allow Cléo to properly develop. Others criticised the film's overly aesthetic style and 'glossiness'. Paule Lejeune, for instance, writes, 'Either one gives in to the charms of actress Corinne Marchand, the image quality in black and white, and the unfamiliar and pleasing scenes in Parisian streets and cafés, or one wonders at the shallowness of the film's intention, its sophisticated atmosphere and framing. Tragedy is absent from this glossy photo album.'[35] But while it is true that Cléo is one of the less ordinary characters in Varda's work, her glamour and extraordinariness reinforce the hiatus between her public image and her real identity. Finally, it is quite remarkable just *how noticeably* Cléo changes in such a short timespan.

Sandy Flitterman-Lewis is the main champion of Varda-as-feminist and devotes a substantial part of her section on Varda and *Cléo de 5 à 7* in her study on women's film-making in France, *To Desire Differently: Feminism and the French Cinema* (1996), to this aspect. She writes, 'Her effort not only to constantly articulate challenges to dominant representations of femininity, but also to express what it means to see – to film – as a woman, means that a profound feminist inquiry is at the centre of all her work.'[36]

Flitterman-Lewis cites *L'Opéra-Mouffe* and *Cléo* as revealing Paris not just in the best realist tradition of New Wave films, but also 'a very precise view of that city, one constructed by a female point of view and fully determined by feminine subjectivity'.[37] Flitterman-Lewis's very thorough and rigorous reading has now become almost universally shared.

Focusing more specifically on the feminism in *Cléo de 5 à 7*, many critics share Flitterman-Lewis's view that the film 'is a surprisingly prescient cinematic exploration of many of the issues concerning women's image and "the gaze". [...] Cléo ceases to be an object, constructed by the looks of men, and is thus empowered with a vision of her own. This evolution from the object to the subject of the gaze, from reflection in a mirror to self-reflection, has important feminist overtones.'[38] However, it is dangerous to assert that Cléo is exclusively an object of the male gaze, given that the only POV shots in the film are female, belonging either to Cléo or Angèle. There is certainly no doubt (particularly when corroborated by interior monologue) that Cléo is mainly the object of Angèle's often patronising gaze. When characters are shown looking at Cléo, Varda makes sure to show us men *and* women. Even in the scene in *Chapter 2* when Cléo is walking down the rue de Rivoli, *women* as well as men are looking at and addressing Cléo. Cléo attracts all eyes, regardless of gender.

In many ways, Flitterman-Lewis's work on *Cléo de 5 à 7* has become the canonical feminist reading, which presents Cléo as an empowered female subject. Jill Forbes has challenged her reading by proposing that, even in the second half of the film, Cléo remains a passive object, a *demi-mondaine*, 'the kind of social being to whom the hours between between 5 p.m. and 7 p.m. traditionally belong'.[39] For Forbes, this is closely entwined, via Cléo's walks, with the *topos* of Paris, a city symbolically likened, in literary criticism, to a whore.[40] Forbes in fact goes so far as to liken Cléo to 'the prostitutes in Balzac's *La Cousine Bette* or Zola's *Nana* [for] she carries her disease within her, all the more virulent for being hidden'.[41] However, Cléo is not a *demi-mondaine*, nor is she a literal 'streetwalker'. Her disease is not venereal. Forbes omits to take into account the wealth of subjective shots that clearly indicate Cléo's position as an *active*, observing subject, something that Flitterman-Lewis identified and analysed in great depth.

However, Flitterman-Lewis's view has recently been espoused by Geneviève Sellier, who, in a chapter about the Left Bank group as the 'feminist' alternative in the New Wave, argues that *Cléo* was perceived as surprisingly novel largely because it was a film made by a woman yet it was 'intellectual' and refused to wallow in sentimentality and character identification.[42] Sellier also proposes that the film's modernity and feminism is a result of Varda being less concerned with sexual alienation than sociocultural alienation: it is Cléo's progression from oppressive popular culture (superstition, feminine 'cliché') to 'real' feelings and 'real' culture (art, Dorothée, cinema, Antoine's curiosity and erudition) that liberates and empowers her.

Varda's view regarding her feminism either in her films or her life is interesting. In a 1975 interview, she was happy to admit that she had come a long way since *Cléo de 5 à 7*, but maintained – and rightly so, in my view – that *Cléo* was nevertheless not a film to be ashamed of in feminist terms: '[...] I don't want to disown *Cléo* for all that. Because *Cléo* expressed – and still expresses in my view – the search for one's identity, and that's the first step towards any kind of feminist intervention.'[43] She claimed many times that she believed herself to be a feminist, which to her means embracing every aspect of being a woman, including pregnancy ('I was on cloud nine'),[44] being a homemaker ('I'm a woman of tomorrow. I have children out of wedlock, advanced ideas, I work hard, all that, but I make my own clothes')[45] and not compromising one's relationship. During the making of *Cléo*, Varda was puzzled by people's expectation that a 'career woman' such as herself should have to sacrifice her personal life and lead a monastic, ascetic life, when in reality, she blended her home life (and burgeoning love affair with Demy) with her professional schedule; she'd meet up with Demy every day and they would take three-year-old Rosalie to the Parc Montsouris.[46] Varda would later repeat this work–life balance by filming *Daguerréotypes* (1975) not just on her street, but only as far as the electric cable for the filming equipment would stretch so that she could keep an eye on her one-year-old son, Mathieu.

Flitterman-Lewis noted that Varda had been given only scant attention (if at all) in most of the British or American accounts of the New Wave. This is correct, but particularly up to the time of writing *To Desire Differently*. James Monaco's book on the New Wave, which in 1990, the year of the first edition of *To Desire Differently*, was the only book of its kind in English, mentions Varda only twice in 372 pages, and then only in relation to the work of other (male) film-makers. This still holds true in a more recent book on the New Wave, a short study guide aimed at undergraduates and laymen, Chris Wiegand's *The Pocket Essential French New Wave*,[47] which sidelines Varda and *Cléo de 5 à 7* by mentioning Varda in relation to Jacques Demy.[48] Regarding *Cléo*, Wiegand writes, 'The film was considerably influenced by *Lola* (Varda was married to Jacques Demy).' While one cannot deny that – as previously mentioned – Varda used a few of the actors from *Lola*, namely Corinne Marchand, Dorothée Blank and Alan Scott, the same set designer, Bernard Évein, and of course the same composer, Michel Legrand, the themes and style of *Cléo* are quite different. Admittedly, *Cléo* is, like *Lola*, a film about waiting, but it is a wait for *something* and not for someone, which is quite different. This sort of comment completely undermines Varda's *auteurist* independence and control. Finally, we could be really pedantic by pointing out that Varda did not marry Demy until early 1962, having met him briefly at the Tours short film festival in 1958, and they did not become better acquainted until the following Tours festival.[49]

However, Varda has received far more attention of late, particularly as the pioneer of the New Wave (something that Jacques Siclier had already observed as early as 1961). Both Michel Marie and Richard Neupert have acknowledged Varda's significant role in early French New Wave history in their respective books, *La Nouvelle Vague: Une école artistique* (1997) and *A History of the French New Wave* (2002). Neupert devotes a third of his second chapter, 'Testing the Water: Alexandre Astruc, Agnès Varda and Jean-Pierre Melville' (pp. 45–72), to *La Pointe courte* as carrying on the tradition of Italian neo-realism and anticipating the New Wave. This said, Neupert nevertheless refrains from including Varda in the 'core' group of the New Wave, but sidelines her by placing her with two more marginal New Wave directors, Astruc and Melville.

Moreover, quite a few books on French cinema history had acknowledged Varda, either in terms of her gender (cf. Colin Crisp)[50] or the pioneering quality of her films; already in 1966, Roy Armes believed *La Pointe courte* was 'an obvious precursor of Alain Resnais's feature films' and classed Varda as an 'intellectual' film-maker alongside Resnais and Marker.[51]

What is fascinating in the early years of the twenty-first century is that French film scholarship, particularly in Britain and the US, has increasingly embraced Varda, largely for the aforementioned pioneering aspect and feminist content of her films, whereas Jacques Demy has become neglected and marginalised. At a pinch, Demy might have been studied as a New Wave film-maker in the early 1990s, at least for *Lola*; nowadays he is considered peripheral to the New Wave at best. Whereas there are English-language chapters and even monographs on Agnès Varda, there is absolutely nothing in English on Demy.

To conclude, there is no doubt that Varda is a feminist film-maker, but as Alan Williams argues, not 'in the sense of making polemical *films à thèse*. She is interested in raising questions but not in answering them.'[52] By leaving so much unresolved, her work, even *Cléo de 5 à 7*, is open to varied and contradictory responses, and this can be frustrating for some feminist scholars, but it can also be very rewarding. In challenging the audience to draw their own conclusions, *Cléo* is typical of a New Wave film, and typical of European art cinema.

Apart from a few exceptions, then, *Cléo de 5 à 7* is now fully accepted as a New Wave film, but with a difference – being the only one made by a woman, its femininity and feminism have been much discussed. It has also received much attention for its uniquely tightly plotted narrative, its Brechtian detached characterisation, its stylistic flourishes and beauty and its openness of meaning, which, as Flitterman-Lewis argues,[53] forces us to emulate Cléo and learn to actively see and think for ourselves.

Notes

1   The Prix Méliès is an annual award for the best French film or French co-production selected by the Syndicat français de la critique de cinéma (French Syndicate of Cinema Critics). In the late 1950s and early 1960s, two films would sometimes win in the same year, for instance Resnais's *Hiroshima mon amour* and Truffaut's *Les Quatre cents coups* in 1959, and Jacques Becker's *Le Trou* and Godard's *À bout de souffle* in 1960.

2   Figures taken from Simsi: *Ciné-Passions: Premier guide chiffré du cinéma en France.*

3   See, for example, Henri Chapier's review, *Combat*, 15 April 1962: 'Praised unanimously by critics, applauded by young Left Bank spectators who were also responsible for the success of so-called New Wave films, soon to be appropriated by the snobbery of the Paris smart set who are terrified of lacking in discernment, and last but not least, selected for the Cannes film festival, *Cléo de 5 à 7* has had a resounding success that even a mainstream film would be proud of.' '*Cléo de 5 à 7 et le péché d'intelligence*'.

4   Duran, Michel, *Le Canard Enchaîné*, 18 April 1962.

5   No. 22, p. 130.

6   Beylie, Claude, 'Le Triomphe de la femme', *Cahiers du cinéma*, pp. 19–28.

7   '[…] in the French film industry, Agnès Varda's shorts sparkle like real gems.' Godard, Jean-Luc, 'Chacun son Tours', *Cahiers du cinéma* 92, February 1959, p. 36.

8   The 1970s and 1980s saw an increase in the number of women directors with Chantal Akerman, Marguerite Duras, Diane Kurys and Coline Serreau. Since the mid-1990s, France has had a high proportion of female directors (about one-third).

9   Aubriant, Michael, 'Un film ambitieux et sévère mais qui peut irriter', *Paris-Presse*, 13 April 1962.

10 Charles Ford thought *Cléo*'s dialogue was too wordy, 'a weakness typical of films which consciously or unwittingly seek to belong to the so-called *cinéma-vérité*'. *Femmes cinéastes ou le triomphe de la volonté* (Paris: Denoël-Gonthier, 1972), p. 112.

11 Uytterhoeven: 'Agnès Varda de 5 à 7', p. 8.

12 Armes, Roy, *French Cinema* (London: Secker and Warburg, 1985), p. 196.

13 Shivas: '*Cléo de 5 à 7* and Agnès Varda', p. 34.

14 Roud, Richard, 'Cléo de 5 à 7', *Sight and Sound* 31.3, Summer 1962, p. 145.

15 Aubriant: 'Un film ambitieux et sévère mais qui peut irriter'.

16 Kauffman, Stanley, *A World on Film* (New York: Harper and Row, 1966), p. 252, quoted in Louise Heck-Rabi, *Women Filmmakers: A Critical Reception* (Metuchen, New Jersey: The Scarecrow Press, 1984), p. 329.

17 Kauffman: *A World on Film*, p. 252.

18 '[…] sans doute promise à la mort …'. Varda: *Cléo de 5 à 7*, p. 9.

19 Aubriant, 'Un film ambitieux et sévère mais qui peut irriter'.

20 This may be quite a normal response. In May 2005, Kylie Minogue's public revelation that she had just been diagnosed with breast cancer spurred a flurry of press attention and interviews. It was reported that she received the news serenely, in contrast to her 'hysterical' parents and boyfriend, Olivier Martinez. 'She was at peace with the news before she even told him.' Benjamin, Laura and Hilary Morgan, 'Kylie exclusive', *Grazia*, 30 May 2005, p. 20.

21 Brown, Royal S., '*Cléo from 5 to 7*', *Cinéaste* 23.4, July 1998, p. 56.

22 Hayward, Susan, 'Beyond the gaze and into *Femme-Filmécriture*: Agnès Varda's *Sans toit ni loi* (1985)', in Susan Hayward and Ginette Vincendeau (eds), *French Film: Texts and Contexts*, 2nd edn (London: Routledge, 2000), p. 269.

23 Kuhn, Annette, *Women's Pictures: Feminism and Cinema*, 2nd edn (London: Verso, 1994), p. 232; Butler, Alison, *Women's Cinema: The Contested Screen* (London: Wallflower, 2002).

24 Dayton, OH: Pflaum Publishing, 1974, pp. 30–34.

25 Metuchen, NJ: The Scarecrow Press, 1984, pp. 322–352.

26 New York: Praeger, 1988, pp. 136–145.

27 Berkeley: University of California Press, 1990, reprinted 1994.

28 New York: Continuum, 1991, pp. 305–309.

29 Bazin, André, *Le Cinéma français de la Libération à la Nouvelle Vague (1945–1958)* (Paris: Éditions de l'Étoile, 1983), p. 194, and Siclier: *Nouvelle Vague?*.
Flitterman-Lewis: *To Desire Differently: Feminism and the French Cinema*, first published 1990, Expanded Edition; Alison Smith, *Agnès Varda* (Manchester: Manchester University Press, 1998), pp. 12–53.

31 Johnstone, Claire, 'Women's Cinema as Counter-Cinema', in Bill Nichols (ed.), *Movies and Methods: An Anthology* (Berkeley: University of California Press, 1976), p. 216.

32 Johnstone: 'Women's cinema as counter-cinema', p. 216.

33 de Beauvoir, Simone, *The Second Sex* (London: Jonathan Cape, 1953), p. 295.

34 Audé, Françoise, *Cinémodèles – Cinéma d'elles* (Lausanne: Éditions de l'âge d'homme, 1981), p. 140.

35 Lejeune: 'Agnès Varda' in *Le Cinéma des femmes: 105 Femmes cinéastes d'expression française*, p. 213.

36 Flitterman-Lewis: *To Desire Differently*, p. 264.

37 Flitterman-Lewis: *To Desire Differently*, p. 264.

38 Flitterman-Lewis: *To Desire Differently*, p. 229.

39 Forbes, Jill, 'Gender and space in *Cléo de 5 à 7*', *Studies in French Cinema* 2.2, 2002, p. 85.

40 Forbes was referring here to Christopher Prendergast's study of *Paris and the Nineteenth Century* (Oxford: Blackwell, 1992), p. 137.

41 Forbes: 'Gender and space in *Cléo de 5 à 7*', p. 87.

42 Sellier, Geneviève, 'Les Francs-tireurs de la Rive gauche: une alternative "féministe"?', *La Nouvelle Vague: un cinéma au masculin singulier* (Paris: CNRS Éditions, 2005), pp. 183–193.

43   Amiel, Mireille, 'Propos sur le cinéma par Agnès Varda', *Cinéma 75*. 204, December 1975, p. 46.

44   Lejeune: 'Agnès Varda', p. 213.

45   Lewis, Flora, 'Varda: is there such a thing as a woman's film?', *New York Times*, Arts and Leisure, 18 September 1977, p. 1, quoted in Acker: *Reel Women*, p. 305.

46   Varda: *Varda par Agnès*, p. 53.

47   Wiegand, Chris, *The Pocket Essential French New Wave* (Pocket Essentials, 2001)

48   Wiegand: *The Pocket Essential French New Wave*, p. 76.

49   Varda: *Agnès*, pp. 26 and 17.

50   Crisp, Colin, *The Classic French Cinema* (Bloomington: Indiana University Press, 1993), p. 209.

51   Armes, Roy, *French Cinema Since 1946: The Personal Style* (London: A. Zwemmer, 1966), p. 101.

52   Williams, Alan, *Republic of Images: A History of French Filmmaking* (Cambridge, Mass.: Harvard University Press, 1992), p. 358.

53   Flitterman-Lewis: *To Desire Differently*, p. 274.

Conclusion

Unlike *La Pointe courte*, *Cléo de 5 à 7* was not so much ahead of its time as very much of its time. Despite Varda's unorthodox incursion into film-making in comparison to her New Wave contemporaries, we have seen that *Cléo* is squarely a New Wave film. Even if its tightly constructed narrative owes a lot to literature, the film is nevertheless as cinematic, topical and dynamic as other New Wave films. In fact, its ethnographic thrust and socio-historical background make it an essential component of that particular school of film-making. Finally, its timeless plot and themes are key to its continued relevance and success.

Any research can yield surprising results. When I started on this book, there were several things that I did not realise. I knew that Agnès Varda was one of the more literary film-makers of the New Wave but I hadn't anticipated spending so much time reading and researching works of literature, and it was very enjoyable to return to one of my former interests. The second revelation, though I already had some inkling of this, was that *Cléo de 5 à 7* is a deceptively simple film. The more closely I examined it, the more meaning I discovered, and the more I was impressed by its precision, its concision and its sophistication. I never tired of viewing it again and again; I always found something new, something different, something I'd missed. As Claudia Gorbman has observed, it really is a hall of mirrors.[1] The third revelation was that, given the subject matter, I expected to feel a little down during my research – cancer, angst, loneliness: these are not cheery issues. Yet, it never depressed me the way some works of art can alter your mood while you are writing about them (in literature, Flaubert's *Madame Bovary*, 1850, or in film, Jean Eustache's *La Maman et la putain*, 1973, are examples that come to mind).

The film is not about death, nor is it really about change, but about a journey, and journeys inevitably mean leaving people (whether friends or family) behind and meeting new ones. That is exactly what Cléo does: she leaves behind old influences in her past and moves on to new acquaintances that better correspond to her new life and persona. Montaigne famously believed that travel is rejuvenating ('les voyages forment la jeunesse') in his essay 'De L'instruction des enfants'. What he meant by this is that travel forces us to reappraise the world and ourselves. The journey itself need not be lengthy or exotic: a walk through Paris, as if seen for the first time, can be equally instructive. In this sense, *Cléo de 5 à 7* is a condensed, filmic and feminine version of the *Bildungsroman*. Through this film, Varda achieved her goal of stimulating the spectator's desire to see, and to see differently.

Note

1   Gorbman: '*Cleo from 5 to 7*: music as mirror', p. 38.

Appendix 1: Film credits

Shot on 35mm film, in 1:66 format, in black and white, except for the credits sequence in Eastmancolor.

Written and directed by: Agnès Varda
Produced by: Georges de Beauregard and Carlo Ponti/Rome-Paris-Films
Assistant directors: Bernard Toublanc-Michel and Marin Karmitz
Director of photography: Jean Rabier
Editing: Jeanine Verneau, assisted by Pascale Laverrière
Original music: Michel Legrand
Lyricist: Agnès Varda
Production design: Bernard Évein, Jean-François Adam and Édith Tertza
Costumes: Alyette Samazeuilh
Sound mixer: Jacques Maumont
Sound technicians: Jean Labussière and Julien Coutelier
Make-up artist: Aïda Carange
Production manager: Bruna Drigo

Cast (by order of appearance):
Cléo Victoire (Corinne Marchand); Irma, the fortune-teller (Loye Payen); Angèle (Dominique Davray); the café owner (Jean Champion); the waiter (Jean-Pierre Taste); the taxi driver (Lucienne Marchand); José, the lover (José Luis de Vilallonga); Bob (Michel Legrand); Plumitif (Serge Korber); Dorothée (Dorothée Blank); Raoul (Raymond Cauchetier); Antoine (Antoine Bourseiller); the doctor (Robert Postec). In the short silent film: Jean-Luc Godard, Anna Karina, Émilienne Mouche, Eddie Constantine, Sami Frey, Danièle Delorme, Yves Robert, Alan Scott, Jean-Claude Brialy.

Appendix 2: Chapter breakdown

(Please note that this is the film's chapter breakdown, not the Criterion DVD breakdown.)

Prologue (17.00 to 17.05) An overhead shot in colour of a table and cards. Madame Irma's off-screen voice as she reads Cléo's cards. Switch to black and white as Cléo and Irma appear on-screen.

Chapter 1 (Cléo from 17.05 to 17.08) Cléo leaves Irma's building and joins Angèle in the 'Ça va ça vient' café. Cléo is upset.

Chapter 2 (Angèle from 17.08 to 17.13) Angèle tells an anecdote while Cléo drinks a coffee. They leave the café and enter a nearby hat shop.

Chapter 3 (Cléo from 17.13 to 17.18) Cléo tries on many hats and buys one. Cléo and Angèle leave and take a taxi. They cross the Seine into the Left Bank while chatting to the female driver.

Chapter 4 (Angèle from 17.18 to 17.25) Continuation of the taxi ride. A diegetic radio news broadcast. Angèle and Cléo arrive home and Cléo changes her clothes and lies down.

Chapter 5 (Cléo from 17.25 to 17.31) Cléo's lover visits her briefly, then her hat is delivered.

Chapter 6 (Bob from 17.31 to 17.38) Bob and Plumitif arrive and play a prank on Cléo. They rehearse for her next album.

Chapter 7 (Cléo from 17.38 to 17.45) After singing a morbid song, Cléo breaks down, changes and leaves the apartment. She walks alone to the nearest café, the Dôme.

Chapter 8 (Some others from 17.45 to 17.52) She enters the Dôme and observes the patrons as she orders a cognac. She leaves and visits Dorothée, who is modelling in a sculpture school.

Chapter 9 (Dorothée from 17.52 to 18.00) Dorothée's modelling session ends and she drives Cléo to her boyfriend Raoul's cinema via Montparnasse station. Cléo confides in her.

Chapter 10 (Raoul from 18.00 to 18.04) Raoul shows the women a short burlesque film.

Chapter 11 (Cléo from 18.04 to 18.12) Dorothée breaks her handbag mirror. They take a taxi and Dorothée gets off while Cléo continues to the Parc Montsouris. She meets Antoine.

Chapter 12 (Antoine from 18.12 to 18.15) Antoine and Cléo talk and he decides to accompany her to the hospital.

Chapter 13 (Cléo and Antoine from 18.15 to 18.30) They walk out of the park and catch a bus to the hospital. Finally, Cléo sees the doctor, who delivers her diagnosis.

Appendix 3: Filmography

7p., cuis., s. de b., ... à saisir (1984)
24 (Twentieth-Century Fox, 2001)
À bout de souffle/Breathless (Jean-Luc Godard, 1960)
Adieu Philippine (Jacques Rozier, 1962)
Amants, Les/The Lovers (Louis Malle, 1958)
Amélie (Jean-Pierre Jeunet, 2001)
Année dernière à Marienbad, L'/Last Year at Marienbad (Alain Resnais, 1961)
Ascenseur pour l'échafaud/Lift to the Scaffold (Louis Malle, 1958)
Baie des anges, La/Bay of Angels (Jacques Demy, 1963)
Bande à part/Band of Outsiders (Jean-Luc Godard, 1964)
Birds, The (Alfred Hitchcock, 1963)
Bonheur, Le/Happiness (1964)
Breakfast at Tiffany's (Blake Edwards, 1961)
Casque d'or/Golden Helmet (Jacques Becker, 1952)
Chien andalou, Un/An Andalusian Dog (Luis Buñuel, 1929)
Citizen Kane (Orson Welles, 1941)
Coup du berger, Le/Fool's Mate (Jacques Rivette, 1956)
Cousins, Les/The Cousins (Claude Chabrol, 1959)
Créatures, Les (1965)
Daguerréotypes (1975)
Demoiselles de Rochefort, Les/The Young Girls of Rochefort (Jacques Demy, 1967)
Du côté de la côte (1958)
Eclisse, L'/The Eclipse (Michelangelo Antonioni, 1962)
Enfants du paradis, Les/Children of Paradise (Marcel Carné, 1945)
Et Dieu ... créa la femme/And God Created Woman (Roger Vadim, 1956)
Femme est une femme, Une/A Woman is a Woman (Jean-Luc Godard, 1961)
French Cancan (Jean Renoir, 1955)
Gaslight (George Cukor, 1944)
Gilda (Charles Vidor, 1946)
Glaneurs et la glaneuse, Les (2000)
Glaneurs et la glaneuse ... deux ans après, Les (2002)
Go-Between, The (Joseph Losey, 1970)
Guerre des boutons, La/The War of the Buttons (Yves Robert, 1962)
Guerre sans nom, La/The Undeclared War (Bertrand Tavernier, 1992)
High Noon (Fred Zinnemann, 1952)
Hiroshima mon amour (Alain Resnais, 1959)
Histoire(s) du cinéma (Jean-Luc Godard, 1988–1998)
Idiot, L' (Georges Lampin, 1946)
It's a Wonderful Life (Frank Capra, 1946)

Jacquot de Nantes (1990)
Jane B. par Agnès V. (1987)
Jeanne Dielman, 23 Quai du Commerce, 1080 Bruxelles (Chantal Akerman, 1976)
Joli Mai, Le (Chris Marker, 1962)
Jules et Jim (François Truffaut, 1962)
Kill Bill, Volumes 1 and 2 (Quentin Tarantino, 2004)
Kung-Fu master! (1987)
Léon Morin Prêtre (Jean-Pierre Melville, 1961)
Lola (Jacques Demy, 1961)
Maigret tend un piège/Maigret Sets a Trap (Jean Delannoy, 1958)
Mépris, Le/Contempt (Jean-Luc Godard, 1963)
Minute pour une image, Une (1982)
Muriel ou le temps d'un retour/Muriel or the Time of Return (Alain Resnais, 1963)
My Life Without Me (Isabel Coixet, 2003)
Notorious (Alfred Hitchcock, 1946)
Notte, La/The Night (Michelangelo Antonioni, 1961)
Ô saisons, ô châteaux! (1957)
Opéra-Mouffe, L' (1958)
Outremer/Overseas (Brigitte Rouän, 1990)
Parapluies de Cherbourg, Les/The Umbrellas of Cherbourg (Jacques Demy, 1964)
Paris nous appartient/Paris Is Ours (Jacques Rivette, 1960)
Petit soldat, Le/The Little Soldier (Jean-Luc Godard, 1960)
Pointe courte, La (1954–1956)
Pulp Fiction (Quentin Tarantino, 1994)
Réponse de femmes (1975)
Quai des brumes/Port of Shadows (Marcel Carné, 1938)
Quatre cents coups, Les/The 400 Blows (François Truffaut, 1959)
Rebel Without a Cause (Nicholas Ray, 1955)
Rope (Alfred Hitchcock, 1948)
Russian Ark (Aleksandr Sokurov, 2002)
Sans toit ni loi/Vagabond (1985)
Sex and the City (HBO, 1998)
Signe du lion, Le/The Sign of Leo (Éric Rohmer, 1959)
Snow White and the Seven Dwarfs (Disney Studios, 1937)
Summer of '42, The (Robert Mulligan, 1971)
Suspicion (Alfred Hitchcock, 1941)
Terms of Endearment (James L. Brooks, 1983)
Thomas Crown Affair, The (Norman Jewison, 1968)
Tirez sur le pianiste/Shoot the Pianist (François Truffaut, 1960)
To Catch a Thief (Alfred Hitchcock, 1954)
Trois places pour le 26 (Jacques Demy, 1988)
Ulysse (1982)
Vivre sa vie/It's My Life/My Life to Live (Jean-Luc Godard, 1962)
Wild One, The (László Benedek, 1954)
Wild Strawberries/Smultronstället (Ingmar Bergman, 1957)

Appendix 4: Selected bibliography

Books

Acker, Ally, *Reel Women: Pioneers of the Cinema 1896 to the Present* (New York: Continuum, 1991), pp. 305–309.

Armes, Roy, *French Cinema Since 1946: The Personal Style* (London: A. Zwemmer, 1966)

Armes, Roy, *French Cinema* (London: Secker and Warburg, 1985).

Audé, Françoise, *Cinémodèles – Cinéma d'elles* (Lausanne: Éditions de l'âge d'homme, 1981).

Baudelaire, Charles, *Les Fleurs du Mal* (Paris: Livre de Poche, 1972)

Bazin, André, 'Agnès Varda: *La Pointe Courte* – Un film libre et pur', *Le Cinéma français de la Libération à la Nouvelle Vague (1945–1958)* (Paris: Éditions de l'Étoile, 1983), pp. 194–195.

Benjamin, Walter, *The Arcades Project*, trans. Howard Eiland and Kevin McLaughlin (Cambridge, Mass.: Harvard University Press, 1999).

Berthomé, Jean-Pierre, *Les Parapluies de Cherbourg de Jacques Demy* (Paris: Nathan, 1995).

Betancourt, Jeanne, *Women in Focus* (Dayton, OH: Pflaum Publishing, 1974), pp. 30–34.

Bogart, Betsy Ann, *Music and Narrative in the French New Wave: The Films of Agnès Varda and Jacques Demy* (Ann Arbor, MI University Microfilms, 2001).

Bordwell, David, *Narration in the Fiction Film* (London: Routledge, 1985).

Branigan, Edward, *Point of View in The Cinema: A Theory of Narration and Subjectivity in Classical Film* (Berlin: Mouton, 1984).

Bruzzi, Stella and Pamela Church-Gibson (eds), *Fashion Cultures: Theories, Explorations and Analysis* (London: Routledge, 2000).

Burch, Noël, *The Theory of Film Practice* (London: Secker and Warburg, 1973).

Cook, Pam (ed.), *The Cinema Book* (London: BFI, 1985).

Crisp, Colin, *The Classic French Cinema* (Bloomington: Indiana University Press, 1993).

Darche, Claude, *Initiation pratique au tarot: Tirages et interprétations divinatoires à la portée de tous* (St-Jean-de-Braye: Dangles, 1992).

Devarrieux, Claire, *Le Cinéma du réel* (Paris: Éditions Autrement, 1988).

Douchet, Jean, *French New Wave* (New York: Distributed Art Publishers, 1999).

Durgnat, Raymond, '*Cléo de 5 à 7*', in Tim Pendergast and Sara Pendergast (eds), *International Dictionary of Films and Filmmakers*, Vol. 1 – Films, 4th edn (Detroit: St James Press, 2000), pp. 253–254.

Estève, Michel, *Agnès Varda* (Paris: Lettres Modernes Minard, 1991).

Falzon, Christopher, *Philosophy Goes to the Movies: An Introduction to Philosophy* (London: Routledge, 2002).

Flitterman-Lewis, Sandy, *To Desire Differently: Feminism and the French Cinema*, expanded edn (New York: Columbia University Press, 1996).

Forbes, Jill, *The Cinema in France After the New Wave* (London: BFI, 1992).

Ford, Charles, *Femmes cinéastes ou le triomphe de la volonté* (Paris: Denoël-Gonthier, 1972).

Fournel, Victor, *Ce qu'on voit dans les rues de Paris* (Paris: Adolphe Delahays, 1858).

Friedberg, Anne, *Window Shopping: Cinema and the Postmodern* (Berkeley: University of California Press, 1993).

Frodon, Jean-Michel, *L'Age moderne du cinéma français: De la Nouvelle Vague à nos jours* (Paris: Flammarion, 1995).

Gleber, Anke, *The Art of Taking a Walk: Flânerie, Literature and Film in Weimar Culture* (Princeton, NJ: Princeton University Press, 1999).

Hayward, Susan, *French National Cinema* (London: Routledge, 1993).

Hayward, Susan and Ginette Vincendeau (eds), *French Film: Texts and Contexts*, 2nd edn (London: Routledge, 2000).

Heck-Rabi, Louise, *Women Filmmakers: A Critical Reception* (Metuchen, NJ: The Scarecrow Press, 1984), pp. 322–352.

Heck-Rabi, Louise, 'Agnès Varda', in Tim Pendergast and Sara Pendergast (eds), *International Dictionary of Films and Filmmakers*, Vol. 2 – Directors, 4th edn (Detroit: St James Press, 2000), pp. 1015–1017.

Kauffman, Stanley, *A World on Film* (New York: Harper and Row, 1966).

Kawin, Bruce F., *How Movies Work* (New York: Macmillan, 1987).

Konigsberg, Ira, *The Complete Film Dictionary* (London: Bloomsbury, 1993).

Kuhn, Annette, *Women's Pictures: Feminism and Cinema*, 2nd edn (London: Verso, 1994).

Kuhn, Annette and Susannah Radstone (eds), *The Women's Companion to International Film* (Berkeley: University of California Press, 1990, reprinted 1994).

Lejeune, Paule, 'Agnès Varda', in *Le Cinéma des femmes: 105 femmes cinéastes d'expression française (France, Belgique, Suisse) 1895–1987* (Paris: L'Atlas/L'Herminier, 1987), pp. 213–216.

Marie, Michel, *La Nouvelle Vague: Une école artistique* (Paris: Nathan Université, 1997).

Nichols, Bill (ed.), *Movies and Methods: An Anthology* (Berkeley: University of California Press, 1976).

Neupert, Richard, *A History of the French New Wave* (Madison: University of Wisconsin Press, 2002).

Pendergast, Tim and Sara Pendergast (eds), *International Dictionary of Films and Filmmakers*, Vols. 1 (Films) and 2 (Directors), 4th edn (Detroit: St James Press, 2000).

Ponikwer, Fiona, *Communicating with the (Un-)dead: A Study of Vampirism as Self-renewal in France – 1850–1900*. Unpublished doctoral thesis, University of East Anglia, 1998.

Prendergast, Christopher, *Paris and the Nineteenth Century* (Oxford: Blackwell, 1992).

Quart, Barbara Koenig, 'Agnès Varda', in *Women Directors: The Emergence of a New Cinema* (New York: Praeger, 1988), pp. 136–145.

Rilke, Rainer Maria, *The Notebook of Malte Laurids Brigge* (1910), trans. John Lindon (Oxford: Oxford University Press, 1984).

Salt, Barry, *Film Style and Technology: History and Analysis*, Second Edition (London: Starword, 1983–1992).

Sartre, Jean-Paul, *Being and Nothingness: An Essay on Phenomenological Ontology*, trans. Hazel E. Barnes (London: Methuen, 1957).

Sartre, Jean-Paul, *Huis clos* (Paris: Folio/Gallimard, 1975).

Siclier, Jacques, *Nouvelle Vague?* (Paris: Éditions du Cerf, 1961).

Simsi, Simon, *Ciné-Passions: Premier guide chiffré du cinéma en France* (Paris: Éditions Dixit, 2000).

Smith, Alison, *Agnès Varda* (Manchester: Manchester University Press, 1998).

Sterrit, David, *The Films of Jean-Luc Godard: Seeing the Invisible* (New York: Cambridge University Press, 1999).

Taboulay, Camille, *Le Cinéma enchanté de Jacques Demy* (Paris: Cahiers du cinéma, 1996).

Tarr, Carrie, with Brigitte Rollet, *Cinema and the Second Sex: Women's Filmmaking in France in the 1980s and 1990s* (London: Continuum, 2001).

Truffaut, François, *Hitchcock by Truffaut: The Definitive Study* (London: Paladin, 1986).

Varda, Agnès, *Cléo de 5 à 7* (Paris: Gallimard, 1962).

Varda, Agnès, *Varda par Agnès* (Paris: Cahiers du cinéma, 1994).

Vincendeau, Ginette, *Stars and Stardom in French Cinema* (London: Continuum, 2000).

Williams, Alan, *Republic of Images: A History of French Filmmaking* (Cambridge, Mass.: Harvard University Press, 1992).

Woolf, Virginia, *Mrs Dalloway* (London: Wordsworth Classics, 1996).

Articles in books, periodicals and newspapers

Amiel, Mireille, 'Propos sur le cinéma par Agnès Varda', *Cinéma* 75.204, December 1975, pp. 36–56.

Anonymous, '*Cléo de 5 à 7*: intelligence et sensibilité', *Démocratie*, 19 April 1962.

Anthony, Elizabeth M., 'From fauna to flora in Agnès Varda's *Cléo de 5 à 7*', *Literature/Film Quarterly* 26.2, 1998, pp. 88–96.

Aubriant, Michel, 'Un film ambitieux et sévère mais qui peut irriter', *Paris-Presse*, 13 April 1962.

Baby, Yvonne, 'Un entretien avec Agnès Varda: "Avec *Cléo de 5 à 7*, j'ai cherché à faire un documentaire subjectif"', *Le Monde*, 12 April 1962.

Biró, Yvette, 'Les Cariatides du temps, ou le traitement du temps dans l'œuvre d'Agnès Varda', Michel Estève (dir.), *Agnès Varda* (Paris: Lettres Modernes, 1991), pp. 41–56.

Boujut, Michel, 'Varda: À vos magnétoscopes!', *L'Évènement du Jeudi*, 26 February 1987, p. 96.

Brown, Royal S., '*Cléo from 5 to 7*', *Cinéaste* 23.4, July 1998, p. 56.

Buck-Morss, Susan, 'The flâneur, the sandwichman and the whore: the politics of loitering', *New German Critique* 39, Autumn 1986, pp. 99–140.

Busnel, Jacques, 'Cent minutes de la vie d'une femme face à l'angoisse de la mort!', *Le Figaro Littéraire*, 12 August 1961.

Caen, Michel and Alain Le Bris, 'Entretien avec Jacques Demy', *Cahiers du cinéma*, May 1964, pp. 1–14.

Chapier, Henri, '*Cléo de 5 à 7* et le péché d'intelligence', *Combat*, 14–15 April 1962.

Chauvet, Louis, 'Cannes: Cléo sur la Croisette', *Le Figaro*, 11 May 1962.

Chazal, Robert, Review, *France-Soir*, 12 April 1962.

Confino, Barbara, interview, *Saturday Review*, 12 August 1972, p. 35.

Constable, Catherine, 'Making up the truth: on lies, lipstick and Friedrich Nietzsche', in Stella Bruzzi and Pamela Church-Gibson (eds), *Fashion Cultures: Theories, Explorations and Analysis* (London: Routledge, 2000), pp. 191–200.

De Baroncelli, Jean, '*Cléo de 5 à 7*', *Le Monde*, 23 April 1962.

Devarrieux, Claire, 'Agnès Varda et le tourniquet du temps', *Le Monde*, 8 January 1986.

Duran, Michel, Review, *Le Canard Enchaîné*, 18 April 1962.

Fabre, Jacqueline, Review, *Libération*, 30 March 1962.

Fieschi, Jean-André and Claude Ollier, 'La Grâce laïque', *Cahiers du cinéma* 165, April 1965, pp. 42–51.

Forbes, Jill, 'Gender and space in *Cléo de 5 à 7*', *Studies in French Cinema* 2.2, 2002, pp. 83–89.

Godard, Jean-Luc, 'Chacun son Tours', *Cahiers du cinéma* 92, February 1959, pp. 31–38.

Gorbman, Claudia, '*Cleo from 5 to 7*: music as mirror', *Wide Angle* 4.4, 1981, pp. 38–49.

Gow, Gordon, 'The underground river', *Films and Filming* 16.6, March 1970, pp. 6–13.

Hayward, Susan, 'Beyond the gaze and into femme-filmécriture: Agnès Varda's *Sans toit ni loi* (1985)', Susan Hayward and Ginette Vincendeau (eds), *French Film: Texts and Contexts*, 2nd edn (London: Routledge, 2000), pp. 269–280.

Johnstone, Claire, 'Women's Cinema as Counter-Cinema', in Bill Nichols (ed.), *Movies and Methods: An Anthology* (Berkeley: University of California Press, 1976), pp. 208–217.

Lacassin, Francis and Yolande Wagner, 'Avec Corinne Marchand de 5 à 7', *Cinéma* 62, June 1962, pp. 61–67.

Lachize, Samuel, '*Cléo de 5 à 7*: (La Beauté Face à la Mort...)', *L'Humanité*, 13 April 1962.

Levitin, Jacqueline, 'Mother of the New Wave: an interview with Agnès Varda', *Women and Film* 1.5/6 (1974), pp. 62–66, p. 103.

Manceaux, Michèle, 'Reportage: Agnès Varda', *L'Express*, 29 June 1961.

Marcabru, Pierre, '*Cléo de 5 à 7* d'Agnès Varda: une lumineuse danse de mort', *Combat*, 11 April 1962.

Mauriac, Claude, Review, *Le Figaro Littéraire*, 14 April 1962.

Mounier, Monique, 'Agnès Varda: "Le Cinéma n'est pas plus difficile pour une femme que pour un homme", *Paris-Presse*, 17 April 1962.

Mouton, Janice, 'From feminine masquerade to flâneuse: Agnès Varda's Cléo in the city', *Cinema Journal* 40.2, Winter 2001, pp. 3–16.

Perez, Michel, '*Cléo de 5 à 7* d'Agnès Varda: la mort l'après-midi', *Le Matin*, 30 January 1986.

Pingaud, Bernard, 'Agnès Varda et la Réalité', *Artsept* 1, January–March 1963, pp. 124–141.

Powell, Nicholas, 'Agnès Varda, the alternative voice', *London Times*, 31 May 1986.

Raynaud, Annette, 'Le Regard d'Agnès Varda', *Artsept* 1, January–March 1963, pp. 121–123.

Revault d'Allonnes, Fabrice, '*Cléo de 5 à 7 et 7 p., cuis., s. de b., à saisir!*', *Cinéma* 336, 8 January 1986, p. 4

Roud, Richard, '*Cléo de 5 à 7*', *Sight and Sound* 31.3, Summer 1962, pp. 145–146.

Roud, Richard, 'The Left Bank', *Sight and Sound*, Winter 1962–1963.

Sellier, Geneviève, 'Les Francs-tireurs de la Rive gauche: une alternative "féministe"?', *La Nouvelle Vague: un cinéma au masculin singulier* (Paris: CNRS Éditions, 2005), pp. 183–193.

Shivas, Mark, '*Cléo de 5 à 7* and Agnès Varda', *Movie*, October 1962, pp. 32–35.

Tailleur, Roger, 'Cléo d'ici à l'éternité', *Positif* 44, March 1962, pp. 15–27.

Uytterhoeven, Pierre, 'Agnès Varda de 5 à 7', *Positif* 44, March 1962, pp. 1–14.

Varda, Agnès, 'Propos sur le cinéma', *Cinéma* 75, pp. 47–48.

Varda, Agnès, 'Agnès Varda de 5 à 7', *Cinématographe* 114, December 1985, p. 21.

Index

7p., cuis., s. de b., ... à saisir
  (1984) 8
À bout de souffle (1960) 5, 6, 7,
  13, 14, 16, 27, 48, 57, 60
Adieu Philippine (1962) 6
Akerman, Chantal 29
Amants, Les (1958) 8
Année dernière à Marienbad, L'
  (1961) 30, 81, 82
Antonioni, Michelangelo 59
Ascenseur pour l'échafaud
  (1958) 60
Assommoir, L' (1876) 28
Astruc, Alexandre 12, 91
Au bonheur des dames (1883)
  59
Audry, Jacqueline 82
Austen, Jane 60
Avignon Theatre Festival 4

Bachelard, Gaston 3, 39
Baie des anges, La (1963) 7
Balasko, Josiane 1
Baldung Grien, Hans 6
Bande à part (1964) 8
Barbaud, Pierre 8
Bardot, Brigitte 7, 9, 72, 73
Baudelaire, Charles 53, 55,
  57–59
Becker, Jacques 8
'Belle P., La' 12, 32, 36–37, 56
Belmondo, Jean-Paul 48
Benedek, László 48, 60

Benjamin, Walter 55, 57
Bergman, Ingmar 82
Birds, The (1963) 73
Blank, Dorothée ix, 7, 71, 90
Bogart, Humphrey 48
Boileau, Nicolas 28
Bonheur, Le (1964) 9, 65, 66,
  67, 70, 87
Bonnaire, Sandrine 65
Bourseiller, Antoine x, 8
Bourvil 7
Brando, Marlon 48, 60
Brassaï 64
Braunberger, Pierre 5
Breakfast at Tiffany's (1961) 8,
  73
Bresson, Robert 9
Brialy, Jean-Claude 8
Bridget Jones: The Edge of
  Reason (2001) 46
Brooks, James L. 85
Brummell, Beau 75
Bruzdowicz, Joanna 8
Buñuel, Luis 14

Cahiers du cinéma 4, 12, 13,
  15, 29, 82
caméra-stylo 12
Camus, Albert 48
Cannes Film Festival 5, 70, 81
Capra, Frank 48
Carné, Marcel 4, 57
Carol, Martine 7

Cartier-Bresson, Henri 64
Casque d'or (1952) 8
Cauchetier, Raymond ix
Centre National de la
    Cinématographie (CNC) 5
Chabrol, Claude 11, 12, 13,
    16, 57
Chien andalou, Un (1929) 14
Ciné-Tamaris 5
cinécriture 12, 14
cinéma de papa 7, 12, 16
Citizen Kane (1941) 22
Cleopatra 9
Coixet, Isabel 85
Constantine, Eddie 8
Coup du berger, Le (1956) 9
Cousine Bette, La (1846) 89
Cousins, Les (1959) 11, 57
Créatures, Les (1965) 8, 66
'Cri d'Amour, Un' ix, 12, 32,
    36–37, 61, 67, 86
Cukor, George 41

Daguerréotypes (1975) 64, 65,
    90
Davray, Dominique ix, 8
de Balzac, Honoré 89
de Beaumarchais, Pierre 74
de Beauregard, Georges 6
de Beauvoir, Simone 88
de Gaulle, General 18
de Givenchy, Hubert 73
de Mérode, Cléo 9
de Montaigne, Michel 95
de Pougy, Liane 9
de Vilallonga, José Luis ix, 8
Dean, James 48, 60
Death Kissing a Maiden 6
Delannoy, Jean 8
Delon, Alain 60
Delorme, Danièle 8

Demoiselles de Rochefort, Les
    (1967) 7, 11
Demy, Jacques 6, 7, 8, 13, 17,
    81, 90, 91
Diderot, Denis 6
Dior, Christian 14, 73
Doisneau, Robert 64
Du côté de la côte (1958) 5,
    71
Dulac, Germaine 82

Eclisse, L' (1962) 59–60
Edwards, Blake 8, 73
Enfants du paradis, Les (1945)
    4
Epstein, Marie 82
Et Dieu… créa la femme
    (1956) 72
Être et le néant, L' (1943) 49
Eustache, Jean 95
Évein, Bernard 10–11, 90

Fabuleux destin d'Amélie
    Poulain, Le (2001) 64
Femme est une femme, Une
    (1961) 7, 8, 11
Fiancés du Pont MacDonald,
    Les 10, 83
Fielding, Helen 46
Flaubert, Gustave 95
French Cancan (1955) 7
Frey, Sami 8

Gaslight (1944) 41
Gay Science, The (1882) 48
Gilda (1946) 45
Glaneurs et la glaneuse, Les
    (2000) 8, 14, 65, 66
Glaneurs et la glaneuse… deux
    ans après, Les (2002) 8
Go-Between, The (1970) 8

Godard, Jean-Luc 5, 6, 7, 8, 9, 11, 12, 13–15, 17, 27, 28, 48, 57, 60, 82
Guerre des boutons, La (1962) 81
Guerre sans nom, La (1992) 17
Guétary, Georges 7
Guy-Blaché, Alice 82

Hayworth, Rita 45
Head, Edith 73
Hedren, Tippy 73
Heidegger, Martin 48
Hepburn, Audrey 8, 73
High Noon (1952) 22, 29
Hiroshima mon amour (1959) 60, 72
Histoire(s) du cinéma (1988–1998) 14
Hitchcock, Alfred 22, 29, 41, 73
Huis-Clos (1944) 53

Idiot, L' (1946) 4
It's a Wonderful Life (1946) 48

Jacques le fataliste (1796) 6
Jacquot de Nantes (1990) 8
Jane B. par Agnès V. (1987) 64
Jaoui, Agnès 1
Jeanne Dielman, 23 Quai du Commerce, 1080 Bruxelles (1976) 29–30
Jewison, Norman 8
Joli mai, Le (1962) 8
Jules et Jim (1962) 45, 81

Karina, Anna 7, 60
Khrushchev, Nikita 18
Kierkegaard, Søren 48
Kill Bill Volumes 1 and 2 (2004) 28

Klein, William 12
Korber, Serge ix,
Kung-Fu master! (1987) 8, 64

Left Bank 4, 5, 13, 27, 63
'Left Bank Group' 12
Legrand, Michel ix, 7, 90
Léon Morin Prêtre (1961) 6
Lola (1961) 6, 38, 90, 91
Losey, Joseph 8
Lumière, Auguste and Louis 65

Madame Bovary (1850) 95
Madonna 15
Maigret tend un piège (1958) 8
Malle, Louis 8, 60
Maman et la putain, La (1973) 95
Marchand, Corinne ix, 6–7, 38–40, 51, 74, 82, 88, 90
Marivaux, Pierre 74
Marker, Chris 8, 12, 13, 81, 91
Mélangite, La 6
Melville, Jean-Pierre 6, 91
'Menteuse, La' 12
Mépris, Le (1963) 7, 72
Minute pour une image, Une (1982) 64
Montfort, Silvia 4
Moreau, Jeanne 7, 8, 39, 45, 59–60
Mrs Dalloway (1925) 62
Mulligan, Robert 8
Muriel ou le temps d'un retour (1963) 17
My Life Without Me (2003) 85

Nana (1880) 89
Nausée, La (1938) 52–53
Nietzsche, Friedrich 48, 76
Noiret, Philippe 4

Notebook of Malte Laurids Brigge (1910) 6, 53
Notorious (1946) 41
Notte, La (1961) 59
nouveau roman 14

Ô saisons, ô châteaux! (1957) 5, 8
Opéra-Mouffe, L' (1958) 5, 7, 8, 14, 17, 64, 66, 71, 88, 89
Ophüls, Max 56
Outremer (1990) 17

Pacifico 7
Parapluies de Cherbourg, Les (1964) 7, 11, 17
Paris nous appartient (1960) 9
Payen, Loye 9
Petit soldat, Le (1960) 17
Piaf, Edith 18
Pointe Courte, La (1954–1956) 4, 5, 8, 14, 65, 66, 67, 71, 91
Polley, Sarah 85
Positif 13, 81
Pride and Prejudice (1813) 60

Quai des brumes (1938) 4
Quatre cents coups, Les (1959) 5, 11, 16, 57

Ray, Nicholas 48
Rebel Without a Cause (1955) 48, 60
Renoir, Jean 7
Réponse de femmes (1975) 88
Resnais, Alain 5, 12, 13, 15, 17, 30, 60, 72, 81, 91
Rilke, Rainer Maria 6, 53
Riva, Emmanuelle 60
Rivette, Jacques 9, 12
Robert, Yves 8, 81

Rohmer, Eric 8, 12, 57
Ronet, Maurice 60
Rope (1948) 22, 29–30
Roquentin, Antoine 52
Rouän, Brigitte 17
Rozier, Jacques 6
Rules, The (1995) 46
Russian Ark (2002) 22

Sand, George 59
Sans toit ni loi (1985) 8, 12, 65, 66, 67
Sartre, Jean-Paul 48–49, 52
Scott, Alan 7, 90
Second Sex, The (1949) 88
Seberg, Jean 7, 48
Second Sex, The (1949) 88
Serreau, Coline 1
Sex and the City (1998) 45
Signe du lion, Le (1959) 8, 57
Snow White and the Seven Dwarfs (1937) 4
Sokurov, Aleksandr 22
Sontag, Susan 15
Summer of '42, The (1971) 8
Suspicion (1941) 41

Tarantino, Quentin 28
Tavernier, Bertrand 17
Terms of Endearment (1983) 85
Théâtre National Populaire (TNP) 4
Thomas Crown Affair, The (1968) 8
Tirez sur le pianiste (1960) 13
To the Lighthouse (1927) 62
Tradition of Quality 13, 16
Trois places pour le 26 (1988) 11

Truffaut, François 5, 11, 12,
    13, 16, 17, 45, 57, 81
Ulysse (1982) 8, 66

Vadim, Roger 72
Vidor, Charles 45
Vilar, Jean 4
Vitti, Monica 59
Vivre sa vie (1962) 8, 28, 60

Warhol, Andy 74
Watteau, Antoine 11, 74
Welles, Orson 22
Wild One, The (1954) 48, 60
Wild Strawberries (1957) 82
Woolf, Virginia 62

Zinnemann, Fred 22
Zola, Emile 28, 59, 89